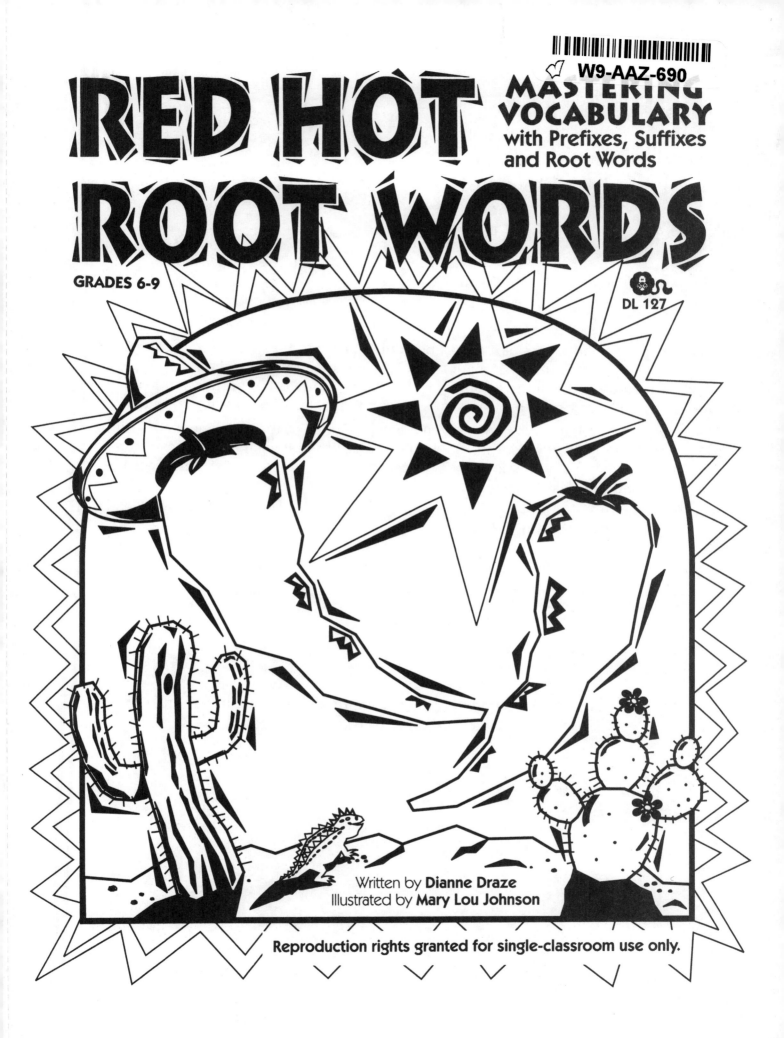

RED HOT ROOT WORDS

GRADES 6-9

MASTERING VOCABULARY
with Prefixes, Suffixes and Root Words

DL 127

Written by **Dianne Draze**
Illustrated by **Mary Lou Johnson**

Edited by **Sonsie Conroy**

Published by **Dandy Lion Publications**

ISBN 1-883055-35-0

Questions regarding this book should be addressed to:
Dandy Lion Publications
3563 Sueldo
San Luis Obispo, CA 93401
805-543-3332

For more information about Dandy Lion products, visit our website
www.dandylionbooks.com

Contents

Root Word Lessons, continued

Suffix Lessons

Why Vocabulary?

You don't need to be a novelist or a lawyer to benefit from a strong command of the English language. Your ability to communicate well directly affects your professional success (regardless of careers) and interpersonal relationships. People who have mastered a wide and varied vocabulary can better present their ideas, convince others of their position, communicate their feelings, and understand what they read.

By building a strong vocabulary students are building the foundation for clear, succinct expression of ideas. An extensive vocabulary gives them the ability to comprehend what they read, write with clarity, grasp the meaning of concepts in all content areas, and express themselves precisely. These are skills that will be advantageous throughout their lives.

English, The Hybrid Language

The English language is a wonderful amalgamation of words from other language, technological innovations, and manufactured terms. The most common, everyday words in the English language are primarily of Anglo-Saxon (originally Germanic) origin, but we have also borrowed terms from the romance languages (Italian and French) and from the Greek and Latin languages. In fact, as our language gets more sophisticated, we are adding more and more non-Germanic words. Of the words that are not Germanic, close to 70% of our vocabulary is derived from Greek and Latin words.

These Latin- and Greek-based words have become the building blocks of modern language. When we need new words to describe medical or technological innovations, we typically combine the appropriate prefixes, root words and suffixes to produce a word that accurately describes the new item or concept. An easily-understood example is *telephone*, derived from the combination of *tele* (distance) and *phon* (sound). Another example is *ecology*, derived from *eco* (house or environment) and *ology* (study of).

By knowing the basis for the words that have been created from these word parts, it becomes easy to recognize and decode terms that have their origins in the Latin and Greek languages.

While there are several approaches to teaching vocabulary, learning the Latin and Greek roots provides a basis for unlocking a wide variety of common, technological, and scientific terms. Once one knows these building blocks, it is easy to ascertain the meaning of a wide variety of words, whether they are presented in a printed or a spoken context.

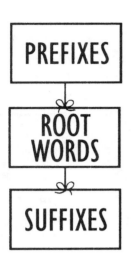

Red Hot Root Words

Red Hot Root Words is an extensive exploration of Greek and Latin prefixes, root words and suffixes. The aim of this book is to present the most frequently-used building blocks in the English language, thereby giving students an arsenal of knowledge that will allow them to decipher words they encounter.

The building blocks are grouped by similar meanings or concepts, thereby giving students both the Latin and Greek words that are related to the same concepts. The object of this book is not to have students learn Latin or Greek, but to become familiar with these building blocks so they can be used in building a larger, richer vocabulary.

The text covers only the most commonly-used terms and the terms that most frequently appear on standardized tests. A more complete list of prefixes, root words, and suffixes appears at the end of each section, giving terms that were not covered, their meanings, and sample words. In this way, you may choose to offer other terms that are not part of the regular lessons if these additional words are more useful to your particular curriculum.

Lesson Notes

In the section called "Lesson Notes" on page 12, you will find a listing of the terms that are covered in each lesson, as well as a list of additional words that use these prefixes, root words or suffixes but are not introduced in the lesson. Some of the words on these lists are easier or more commonly-used words than those introduced in the lessons, and some are more difficult or obscure words. With these lists you can adapt your vocabulary lessons to the abilities of your students, giving some students easier words and some students more demanding words. You can also use these words to introduce your lessons or words for extension exercises or tests.

Lessons

Each lesson introduces at least two prefixes, root words or suffixes. The word parts in each lesson have the same or related meanings, which are reflected in the lesson's title. The lessons are presented in the following way:

- The top part of each lesson introduces these word parts, gives their meanings, and provides sample words that should be familiar to students. By knowing what these familiar words mean, it is easier for students to unlock the meanings of words that use the same word stems.
- The bottom part of the first page of the lesson presents ten words, their parts of speech, their definitions, and sentences.

* The second page of each lesson is a worksheet that gives students practice in defining and using the ten vocabulary words. The worksheets ask students to select the correct word to complete the sentence, match the words with definitions, find the synonyms or antonyms for the vocabulary words, answer questions that reflect the words' usages, build charts, and complete analogies. Each of the ten words is used at least once in the exercises.

What words do I want my students to learn?

Decisions Before You Start

If you present one lesson from the book each week, you will have more than a year's worth of lessons. For this reason, you may want to select those lessons that you think are most important for your students to know. Depending on grade level or curriculum focus, some word stems may be more worthwhile than others.

Likewise, you should probably decide before you start your vocabulary study whether your emphasis will be on learning the word stems, which would give students a generalized knowledge base for decoding unfamiliar words, or whether you want students to master specific new vocabulary words (like the ten words presented in each lesson or some additional words of your choosing). The latter would allow them to comprehend the word stems for future application and also add to their present vocabulary.

Practice GAMES Applications

Doing More

You can make the presentation of root words as simple or extensive as you want. The words and exercises that are presented on the two pages of each lesson could be your entire vocabulary lesson but they could be just a starting point. There are several other things that you can and should do to reinforce understanding of the word stems and associated vocabulary words.

See the next section entitled "Additional Lesson Ideas" for other activities you can do to provide additional or different forms of practice. This section presents ideas for introducing the words, ways to provide practice, and games to make vocabulary study fun.

Introducing The Words
■ Deducing Meanings

Show the class several words with a given root or affix (suffix or prefix) that you will be studying. Choose familiar words that you are sure students have encountered previously. Ask, "What do these words have in common?" After they have stated the common quality, introduce the suffix, root word or prefix, its meaning and any derivations of its spelling. Then introduce the vocabulary words that are formed from this base.

■ Does Anyone Recognize This Word Base?

Before introducing a word base or the vocabulary words related to the affix or root word, write the term on the board, discuss its meaning, and ask students to supply words that they think are derived from this word. Give them a couple of days to add words to the list.

A word of caution: Not all words that include the particular affixes or root word are derived from the Latin or Greek base word. For example, while "du" means "two" and is the prefix used in words like duplex, duplicate and duo; duress, which also starts with "du," is derived from a French term for oppression, and dubious is derived from an English term for doubt. Students should check the meaning and word history of their words in a reliable dictionary before adding them to the list.

■ Dissecting The Word

As a new word is presented, ask students to separate the word into prefix, root word and suffix. Then look at the word parts and their meanings and speculate what the vocabulary word that is derived from these word parts means.

Example:
procession = pro + cess + ion
pro = forward
cess = go
ion = the act of
procession - the act of going forward

monograph = mono + graph
mono = one
graph = write
monograph - written article on one subject

Gaining Ownership
■ Using Words in Their Own Writing

Students won't "own" words until they can incorporate them in their speech or writing. Once they comprehend the meaning of a word, the next step is to apply this information by using the word in a sentence. Ask students to write a sentence for each vocabulary word.

■ Combining Building Blocks Chart

Make a chart using the outline on page 26 that lists prefixes along one side and root words along the top. Ask students to write words in the center squares that are combinations of the prefixes and root words. Not every square will contain a word.

■ Synonyms and Antonyms

By looking at synonyms and antonyms, you not only reinforce the meaning of words but you introduce a larger vocabulary than the list of ten weekly words would provide.

After you have introduced the vocabulary words each week, ask students to find synonyms and antonyms for the words. They may not be able to readily find synonyms and antonyms for every vocabulary word, but some words have a long list of words with similar or different meanings. On a chart or portion of the board, list words and their synonyms and antonyms.

■ Partner Writing

This exercise gives students a double opportunity to apply their knowledge of the vocabulary words and how they are used in speech.

Have students work in partners for this exercise. Ask each person to write sentence. Ask each person to write sentences for each vocabulary word, inserting blanks where the words would appear. The sentences should be in a random order, not in the order in which the words appear on the worksheet. Students should then exchange papers and fill in the blanks on their partners' papers with the vocabulary words.

■ Word Study

Ask each student to select two words from the vocabulary list and do a complete word study for that word. Their written presentation should include the following:

- the word
- a definition
- antonyms and synonyms
- the word derivation
- related words (other word forms)

Use the worksheet on page 25.

■ Sentence Completion

Give students the beginnings of sentences that include the vocabulary words and ask them to complete the sentences in ways that reflect the meaning of the word.

Example:
He showed his remorse by . . .
The doctor's prognosis . . .
The corpulent cat . . .

■ Monthly Review

After several weeks have passed and students have been introduced to a variety of word bases, provide a review in one of two ways:

- **Categorization** - Give students a list of words from several different lessons. Ask them to put the words in groups with common meanings. Then have them add one or two more words to each category.
- **Application** - Select words from the lists of extra words; that is, words with word bases you have studied but were not the ten words that were presented in the lessons. See if students can apply their knowledge of prefixes and root words by giving the word base and its meaning. Ask them to provide an educated guess as to the meaning of the new word. Say something like, "If *retro* means back, what does *retroflection* mean?"

■ Internet Practice

The Internet offers many educational opportunities. One site that specializes in presenting vocabulary based on Latin and Greek root words is Vocabulary University. In addition to on-line puzzles that change periodically, students can submit their original stories. The web address is:

http://www.vocabulary.com

Check the Internet periodically for other educational sites that present an opportunity to learn or practice vocabulary skills.

The Grammar Connection

■ Adjective - Adverb

The descriptive words that are given in each lesson are adjectives, not adverbs. Students should know, however, that there are adverbial equivalents for almost all adjectives. Discuss the following:

- Adjectives describe nouns, and adverbs describe verbs and adjectives.
- Many adverbs, though not all, are formed by adding "ly" to the end of the word.

Ask students to find the adverb that is associated with each adjective and use it in a sentence, either by writing a sentence or reading and acting it out.

■ Parts of Speech

One advantage of learning to unlock the building blocks that comprise words is that when you have mastered the meaning of one word, you are able to unlock the meaning of its several grammatical forms. Many words have several different forms. By adding different suffixes, a word can be used as a noun, a verb, an adjective, or an adverb. Use the chart on page 27 to have students look at the different forms of a word. To complete the chart, you will fill in three prefixes and three root words in the first (left) column. For each prefix and root word, students should choose a word that uses that prefix or root and write the form of the word as a verb, an adjective, an adverb, and a noun. Here are two examples:

root word - *trib,* meaning *pay*
verb - contribute
adjective - contributive, contributory
adverb - contributively
noun - contribution, contributor

prefix - *re*, meaning *again*
verb - reverse
adjective - reversible
adverb - reversely, reversibly
noun - reversion, reversal

Creative Applications
■ Cinquain Poetry

Some words are appropriate starting points for writing cinquain poems. Ask students to choose a word and use the following format for writing a poem that describes the word. It works best if the chosen word is a noun. If many of your words are verbs or adjectives, allow students to select the noun form of one of the words. For example, choose "dictator" instead of "dictate" or "dictatorial."

Cinquain Format
line 1:   chosen word
line 2:   two descriptive words
line 3:   three action or "ing" words
line 4:   four related words
line 5:   one or two words that restate the
          subject

■ Word Posters

Have students choose a word from the vocabulary list, from the list of related words, or from words that they have found that are derived from the base word. Then have them create a poster that illustrates the word. The poster should have the following characteristics:

* the chosen word written in large letters at the top
* the part of speech
* a short definition
* a sentence that uses the word in context
* a large picture that illustrates the word or the way it is used in the sentence.

■ Headlines

First ask students to study headlines in the local newspaper. Note how the headlines use graphic language that will attract the readers' attention in a glance.

Each week as you go through the vocabulary words, discuss which verbs would be suitable for headlines. In groups of three or four, have students brainstorm possible headlines. Chose the best ones and write them on strips of paper or on a chart. Add to your collection each week.

Games
■ Concentration

Prepare two cards for each vocabulary word, one that has the vocabulary word written on it and one that has the part of speech and definition on it. Mix up the cards and turn them upside down or tape them on the wall with the writing facing toward the wall.

Have students take turns turning over two cards, trying to match each word with its correct definition. If two cards are matched, they can be turned upright and the person or team who made the correct match gets a point.

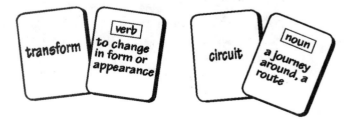

■ Categories

This is a fun game to play as a review every couple of weeks. You need to have more than one week's worth of words to make this worthwhile.

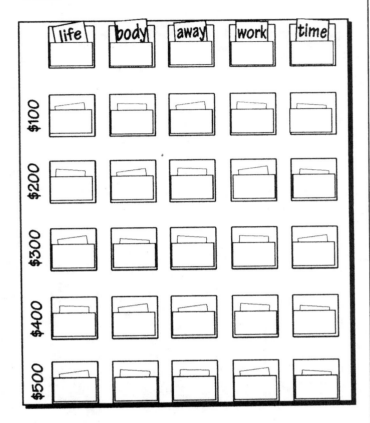

Prepare a board that has five columns horizontally and five rows vertically. Put colored pockets along the top. In these pockets you will put descriptions of your categories. These categories will be the definitions of the word parts you have studied. They will be words like "life," "body," "away."

Along the left side, put money amounts ($100 to $500) for each row. Then put five pockets in each row so that they fall under the pockets at the top.

Choose five vocabulary words for each category, and prepare an index card for each word. On the card write the word and the definition. Place the easy words in the top part of the chart (next to $100 and $200) and the hardest words at the bottom (next to $500).

To play the game, first divide the class into teams. When it is a student's turn he or she will tell you what category and how much money he or she wants. You will draw the card out of that pocket and read the definition. The student will provide the answer by stating, "What is___?" (giving the word that matches the definition). If the answer is correct, that team gets the amount of money that was selected and another turn.

■ Guess-a-Word

This game should also be played after you have completed several lessons and have a backlog of words with which to work.

Prepare strips that have five to ten vocabulary words on them. Since this is played with two teams, each team should have a strip that has different words on it than the one their opponents are using.

Students on one team start with the first word on the top of their list. Providing single-word clues, one team member tries to help the other members guess what the word is without actually saying the word. Once the word has been guessed, a point is scored and they can move on to the next word. If the correct word is not provided within the time limit (you can set a limit appropriate to your students' abilities), the other team gets a turn with their list of words.

■ Add One

Divide the class into two teams. Read or write on the board three words that are derived from the same word base. Give one team (either on an alternating basis or by selecting the team that raises a hand first), a chance to provide (without prompts, dictionaries or word lists), another word that is derived from this same word base. Write the word on the board and give this team a point. Then give the other team a chance to provide a word. When no other words can be added, start a new round with a different set of three words.

Lesson Notes

Lesson 1 - Over and Under

This lesson introduces the following prefixes:

sub - below, under
trans - across, over

Other Words with These Prefixes

subdivide	transfigure
subject	transfuse
submerge	transgress
submission	transient
submissive	transitory
subordinate	translate
subsequent	transmigrate
substitute	transmit
subversive	transparent
subway	transpose
transaction	transverse

Lesson 2 - More, More, More

This lesson introduces the following prefixes:

hyper - above, over, more
super, supr, sur - above, over, more

Other Words with These Prefixes

hyperactive	superpower
hypersensitive	superstition
superabundant	superstructure
superb	supremacy
supersede	surmount
superhuman	surpass
superimpose	surveillance
superintendent	survey
superiority	survive

Lesson 3 - Before and After

This lesson introduces the following prefixes:

fore - before, toward
post - after, behind
pre - before, toward

Other Words with These Prefixes

foreshadow	postmortem
foresight	precipitate
forestall	precocious
foretell	prejudice
postdate	premonition
posterity	presume

Lesson 4 - Backward and Forward

This lesson introduces the following prefixes:

pro - forward, before
retro - backwards

Other Words with These Prefixes

proboscis	prohibit
procession	project
proclivity	projectile
procreate	proliferate
productivity	propel
profane	proportion
proficient	prorate
profile	prospect
profound	retroflection
profuse	retrospection
program	

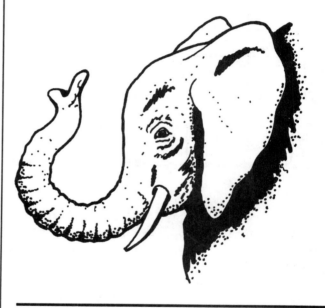

Lesson 5 - Around and Around

This lesson introduces the following prefixes:

cir, circum - around
peri - around, surrounding, near *

Other Words with These Prefixes

circuitous	circumspect
circuitry	circumstantial
circulate	circumvention
circulation	peripheral
circumambulate	periodontal
circumpolar	peristalsis
circumscribe	

* Many words using the *peri* prefix are scientific terms.

Lesson 6 - Ways to Move

This lesson introduces the following prefixes:

ad - to, toward
re - back, again
se - apart, away

Other Words with These Prefixes

adaptation	repetition
adjunct	resume
administer	retort
advertise	retract
advocate	retreat
rebound	retribution
redundant	revive
refurbish	secede
regain	seclusion
regression	secrete
rehearsal	secretive
reorganize	sedition
repel	seduce

Lesson 7 - Coming Through

This lesson introduces the following prefixes:

dia - through, across
per - through, across

Other Words with These Prefixes

dialogue	permeate
dialect	permutation
dialysis	perpendicular
diatribe	perpetrate
per capita	perpetual
perception	perspective
perennial	perspire
permeable	pervious

Lesson 8 - Outside

This lesson introduces the following prefixes:

e, ec, ef, ex - out of, outside
extra, exter - out of, outside, excessive

Other Words with These Prefixes

efficiency	extinguish
effluent	extort
evoke	extract
exception	extradite
expel	extraneous
expire	extrapolate
export	extricate
expunge	extrovert
extinct	exuberant

Lesson 9 - All Together

This lesson introduces the following prefixes:

co, col - with, together
com, con - with, together
sym, syn - with, together

Other Words with These Prefixes

collate	convene
communal	correlate
comply	symbiosis
confederation	symphony
conformity	symposium
conglomerate	synchronize
congress	syncopation
congruent	syndicate
coincide	synergy
coincident	synthesis
coincidental	synthetic

Lesson 10 - Moving Away

This lesson introduces the following prefixes:

ab, abs - away, from
apo - away, from

Other Words with These Prefixes

abbreviate	absentee
abeyance	abstinence
abhor	apocalypse
abject	apologize
abolition	apoplexy
abrasion	apostle
abrogate	apothecary
abscond	

Lesson 11 - Against

This lesson introduces the following prefixes:

ant, anti - against
contra, counter - against
ob - against, facing

Other Words with These Prefixes

antarctic	contradict
antibiotic	contrary
antibody	counteract
anticlimactic	counterintelligence
antidote	oblivious
antigen	obsolete
antithesis	obstruct
contraband	obtuse

Lesson 12 - Numbers 1 - 4

This lesson introduces the following prefixes:

mono, uni - one
bi, du - two
tri - three
quad, quar - four

Other Words with These Prefixes

bifocal	quadruplet
bilateral	quarterly
dual	quartet
duplicate	triceratops
monocracy	tricolor
monolith	trident
monologue	trimester
monotone	triptych
quadrant	triune
quadriceps	unification
quadrille	unilateral
quadruped	unique

Lesson 13 - Numbers 5 - 10

This lesson introduces the following prefixes:

penta, quint - five
sex, hexa - six
sept, septem - seven
oct, octo - eight *
nov, non - nine *
dec, deci, deca - ten

Other Words with These Prefixes

decagon	nonagenarian
decagram	nonagon
decibel	octoped
deciliter	quintessence
decimal	quintuple
decimate	septenary
hexapod	sexagenarian
hexagonal	
hexameter	

* Students will undoubtedly notice that the months of October and November are derived from the prefixes for eight and nine, while they are the tenth and eleventh months. This is because when these months were named in the original calendar, they were the eighth and ninth months. Later two months (July and August, in honor of Julius and Augustus Caesar) were added to the calendar, and these two months retained their names but became the tenth and eleventh months.

Lesson 14 - Beside, Between and Among

This lesson introduces the following prefixes:

epi - on, beside, among
inter - between, among
para - beside, among

Other Words with These Prefixes

epicenter	intermission
epigram	internal
epigraph	interrogate
epitaph	intervene
epitome	paradigm
intercept	paradox
interior	paragon
interject	paralegal
intermediate	parallelogram
intermingle	paranoid

Lesson 15 - Down and Away

This lesson introduces the following prefixes:

cata - down, away from
de - down, away from
tele - far, distance

Other Words with These Prefixes

catalogue	demerit
catapult	depress
cataract	deprive
debunk	deride
decadence	telecast
deduct	telekinesis
deflate	telescopic
defunct	televise
demean	

Lesson 16 - In and Into

This lesson introduces the following prefixes:

em, en - in, into, with
im, in - in
intro, intra - in, into

You will note that the prefixes *im* and *in* are also introduced in lesson 18 with the meaning *not*.

Other Words with These Prefixes

embrace	imbue
embroider	immanent
embryo	immerse
empathy	immigrate
emperor	impart
emphatic	impeach
empire	impede
empower	impersonate
encapsulate	impulsive
enclave	infuse
encourage	inhabitant
endanger	inherit
endemic	inhibit
enduring	injunction
engulf	innovate
ennoble	intravenous
ensue	introject
environment	

Lesson 17 - The Size of Things

This lesson introduces the following prefixes:

mega - large, great
multi - many
poly - many
semi, hemi - half

Other Words with These Prefixes

hemispheroid	multistage
megalomania	multitudinous
megalosaur	polygamy
megapode	polynomial
multifold	semiannual
multimedia	semiautomatic
multiplex	semicolon
multiplicative	semiconductor
multiplicity	semifinal
multipurpose	

Lesson 18 - Just Not

This lesson introduces the following prefixes:

a, an - not
il, ir - not
im, in - not
non - not

Please note that the prefixes *im* and *in* are also introduced in lesson 16 with the meaning *in*.

Other Words with These Prefixes

anarchy	inanimate
anomaly	inarticulate
apathy	incognito
illegible	inhospitable
immobilize	irrelevant
immoral	irrevocable
immortal	nonchalant
impatient	nondescript
impractical	nonexistent
inaccessible	nonpartisan
inadmissable	

Lesson 19 - Bringing and Building

This lesson introduces the following root words:

port - bring, carry
stru, struct - build

Other Words with These Roots

constructive	porter
infrastructure	portfolio
instructor	portray
obstruction	reconstruction
portage	report
	support

Lesson 20 - Ways of Writing

This lesson introduces the following root words:

gram, graph - write, writing
scrip, scrib - write, writing

Other Words with These Roots

ascribe	graphology
biography	holograph
circumscribe	manuscript
diagram	phonograph
epigraph	photograph
geographer	scribe
grammar	scripture
gramophone	telegraph
graph	transcription

Lesson 21 - Reaching the End

This lesson introduces the following root words:

fin - end
sat - enough
term - end

Other Words with These Roots

affinity	satiety
determination	satire
dissatisfaction	satisfaction
financial	satisfactory
finial	saturation
finite	terminally
infinitesimal	terminus
satiate	unsatisfactory

Lesson 22 - Father, Mother, Birth

This lesson introduces the following root words:

gen - *birth*
mater, matri - mother
pater, patr - father

Other Words with These Roots

gene	matricide
generation	matrilineal
gender	matron
generate	paternity
generic	patriarch
generosity	patrilineal
geniality	patrimony
genocide	patriotism
genteel	patron
maternal	patronize
matriarchy	

Lesson 23 - All Things Great and Small

Like lesson 17 in the prefix section, this lesson covers words that relate to size, both large and small. The following root words are introduced:

magn, magni - great
maxi - large, great
micro - small
min - small

Other Words with These Roots

diminish	microcosm
Magna Carta	micrometer
magnanimity	microscope
magnification	minify
magnify	minimal
magnitude	miniature
magnum opus	minor
maxim	minuet
microfilm	minute

Lesson 24 - All About Work

This lesson introduces the following root words:

labor - work
oper - work
techni - skill
trib - pay, bestow

Other Words with These Roots

architect	operative
attribute	operational
contribute	redistribute
distributive	technicality
laboratory	technicolor
labored	technique
labor-saving	technocracy
opera	tributary

Lesson 25 - Just Asking

This lesson introduces the following root words:
quir, quis - ask
quer, ques - ask
rog - ask, seek

Other Words with These Roots

interrogation	query
interrogative	questionable
interrogator	questionnaire
prerequisite	requisition
querulous	

Lesson 26 - Life and Death

This lesson introduces the following root words:

mori, mort - death
nat - birth
vit, viv - life

You may want to combine or precede with lesson 22 that offers the root word *gen* that means *birth* or *origin*. You may also want to follow up with lesson 28 that includes the word *bio*, meaning *life*.

Other Words with These Roots

convivial	nationalize
immortality	native
morgue	nativity
mortality	naturalize
mortgage	revitalize
moribund	revive
mortician	vital
mortuary	vitality
natal	vitamin

Lesson 27 - Earth and Sea

This lesson introduces the following root words:

aqua, aqui - water
geo - land, earth
hydr - water
mar, mer - sea
terr - land, earth

Other Words with These Roots

aquamarine	hydrometer
aquarium	marinade
aqueous	mariner
aquiculture	mermaid
aquifer	submarine
geocentric	subterranean
geode	terrace
geologist	terrain
geometry	terrier
geothermal	territorial
hydraulic	territory
hydrodynamics	

Lesson 28 - Some Body Words

This lesson introduces the following root words:

bio - life
carn - body, flesh
corp - body

Other Words with These Roots

bioethics	corporeal
biological	corps
biopsy	corpse
biorhythm	incarnation
carnivore	incorporate
corporal	reincarnation

Lesson 29 - Body Parts

This lesson introduces the following root words:

cap, capit - head
cor, cour, cord, card - heart
man - hand
ped, pod - foot

Other Words with These Roots

accord	discord
capable	emancipate
capital	encouraged
capitalism	expedient
captivate	impede
captor	manacle
cardiology	manual
cardiovascular	manufacture
centipede	manuscript
concordance	pedestal
coronary	pedigree
courage	podiatry
courageous	recapitulate
courteous	tripod

Lesson 30 - Moving

This lesson introduces the following root words:

curr, curs - run, course
grad, gress - move forward, step
mob, mot, mov - move

Other Words with These Roots

automobile	gradual
congress	graduate
curriculum	immovable
cursive	mobilization
cursor	motive
demote	precursor
digression	progression
egress	recurrent
emotion	retrograde
excursion	transgress
gradient	transgression

Lesson 31 - Look and See

This lesson introduces the following root words:

scop - see, look
spec, spic - see, look
vis, vid - see, look

Other Words with These Roots

despicable	species
evident	specify
gyroscope	spectacle
inspect	spectacular
inspector	spectator
invisible	spectroscope
microscope	speculation
periscope	speculative
perspicacity	stethoscope
prospect	videographer
providential	visa
provision	visionary
revise	visualize

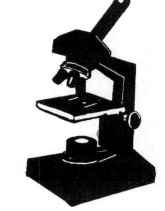

Lesson 32 - Speaking

This lesson introduces the following root words:

dic - say, declare
loc, log, loqu - speak, talk
ora - speak
test - bear witness

Other Words with These Roots

colloquial	monologue
contest	neologism
contradict	oracle
dictation	oration
diction	orator
edict	predict
elocution	protest
epilogue	soliloquy
indicative	testament
indict	testimony
malediction	verdict

Lesson 33 - Sound Words

This lesson introduces the following root words:

aud - hear
phon - sound
son - sound

Other Words with These Roots

audience	resonance
audiology	saxophone
audiophile	sonata
audit	soniferous
auditorium	sonometer
cacophony	symphonic
dissonant	symphonious
inaudible	xylophone
megaphone	
phonetically	

Lesson 34 - The Shape of Things

This lesson introduces the following root words:

cycl - circle
orb - orbit, circle
rect - straight
sphere - sphere

Other Words with These Roots

biosphere	direct
correct	directness
cyclist	encyclopedia
cycloid	rectifiable
Cyclops	rectilinear
cyclorama	spheroid
cyclotron	stratosphere

Lesson 35 - Strength and Power

This lesson introduces the following root words:

dyna, dynamo - power
fort, forc - strong
pot - power
vali, valu - strength, worth

Other Words with These Roots

comfort	potentate
dynamometer	potentially
dynastic	valiancy
effortless	valiant
equivalent	validate
forte	validity
fortification	valuation
fortress	valueless
impotent	

Lesson 36 - It's About Time

This lesson introduces the following root words:
ann, enn - year
chron - time
dai, dia - day
jour - day
tempo - time

Other Words with These Roots

adjourn	du jour
anachronism	journal
annals	journey
bicentennial	per annum
chronograph	synchronous
chronology	temporal
contemporaneous	

Lesson 37 - Twisting and Turning

This lesson introduces the following root words:
rot - turn, wheel
tort, tors - twist
vers, vert - turn

Other Words with These Roots

advertise	rotisserie
avert	rotogravure
contortion	rotor
contortionist	rotund
controversial	rotunda
convert	tortuous
distortion	transverse
extortion	verse
invert	version
reversible	versus
revert	vertebra
rotary	vertigo

Lesson 38 - Thinking and Remembering

This lesson introduces the following root words:

intellect, intellig - power to know
mem - remember
sens - think, perceive, feel

Other Words with These Roots

commemoration	sensational
insensitive	sensible
intellect	sensory
intelligentsia	sensuous
memorabilia	sentient
memorable	sentiment
memorandum	sentinel
memorial	sentry
memorize	unintelligible

Lesson 39 - Going, Going, Gone

This lesson introduces the following root words:

ced, cess - go, withdraw, separate
ceed, cede - go, yield
migr - wander

Other Words with These Roots

accessible	intercession
accession	migrant
accessory	migration
ancestor	procedure
antecedent	processional
cede	recession
cessation	recessional
concession	recessive
emigration	secession
immigration	success
intercede	

Lesson 40 - Take a Stand

This lesson introduces the following root words:

sist - stand
sta stab, stat - stand

Other Words with These Roots

establish	station
persist	statistic
stabilize	status
stadium	status quo
stamen	statutory
stance	subsist
stanza	

Lesson 41 - Touching and Holding

This lesson introduces the following root words:

tact, tang - touch, feel
tag, tig - touch
ten, tin, tain - hold

Other Words with These Roots

abstain	tactful
abstinence	tactics
contain	tactless
container	tangential
detain	tenable
intact	tenement
intangible	tenacity
lieutenant	tenancy
maintain	tenuous
retention	tenure
sustenance	

20

Lesson 42 - Governmental Words

This lesson introduces the following root words:

crac, cracy - rule, power
dom - rule, power
feder, fid - faith, trust

Other Words with These Roots

autocratic	domineering
bona fide	federalism
bureaucracy	fiduciary
bureaucrat	infidelity
confederacy	predominant
confident	plutocracy
confide	technocracy
domain	theocracy
dominant	

Lesson 43 - People

This lesson introduces the following root words:

dem, demo - people
greg - group, crowd
hum - man
pop - people

Another root word that you may want to introduce with this lesson is the word *anthro*, meaning *human being*.

Other Words with These Roots

aggregation	pandemic
democrat	philanthropist
depopulate	popularity
egregious	popularize
endemic	populate
epidemic	populist
humanity	
inhumane	

Lesson 44 - Able and Capable

This lesson introduces the following suffixes:

able, ible - able, can do
il, ile - capable of being, like

Other Words with These Suffixes

agile	manageable
agreeable	permissible
audible	reliable
bearable	senile
combustible	sociable
fertile	sterile
forcible	transferable
fragile	unthinkable
imbecile	versatile
juvenile	visible
laudable	

Lesson 45 - It's Like

This lesson introduces the following suffixes:

al - like, pertaining to
ine - like, pertaining to
ous - like, pertaining to

Other Words with These Suffixes

cerebral	obnoxious
covetous	optional
decimal	oral
feminine	porcine
fortuitous	prejudicial
gaseous	pugnacious
gracious	rapacious
gradual	spiritual
homogeneous	superficial
infamous	supine
intellectual	synonymous
internal	tedious
judicial	tortuous
manual	venomous
mental	vicarious
mysterious	zealous
oblivious	

Lesson 46 - More Like Words

This lesson introduces the following suffixes:

ic - like, pertaining to
ical - like, pertaining to
ive - like, pertaining to

Other Words with These Suffixes

abusive	explosive
accumulative	geological
aggressive	hieroglyphic
artistic	historical
assertive	metabolic
captive	metallic
collective	methodical
cooperative	nomadic
comical	paradoxical
commemorative	patriotic
creative	poetic
cubical	rhetorical
derogative	metabolic
descriptive	spherical
dramatic	strategic
emphatic	symbolic
eruptive	theatrical
ethical	toxic
exhaustive	volcanic
expletive	

Lesson 47 - With and Without

This lesson introduces the following suffixes:

ful - full of
less - without
ose, ous - full of, excessive

Other Words with These Suffixes

beautiful	nameless
bountiful	peerless
careless	perilous
colorful	plentiful
fitful	populous
friendless	rapturous
frightful	regardless
glamorous	religious
gracious	shameful
harmless	sorrowful
hopeless	stupendous
lifeless	tireless
meticulous	varicose

Lesson 48 - Resembling

This lesson introduces the following suffixes:

ish - resembling, like
ly - resembling, like
oid - resembling, like
some - resembling, like

Other Words with These Suffixes

alkaloid	partly
burdensome	selfish
celluloid	schizoid
childish	sheepish
duly	sleepily
feverish	spirally
ghoulish	trapezoid
gravely	typhoid
humanoid	wholesome
lithesome	worrisome
lonely	yellowish
lovely	

Lesson 49 - Conditional Words

This lesson introduces the following suffixes:

acy - condition
tude - condition
ure - condition

Other Words with These Suffixes

altitude	overture
delicacy	papacy
fallacy	piracy
fortitude	posture
gratitude	procedure
latitude	rectitude
legacy	rupture
legislature	servitude
literature	temperature
longitude	tenancy
magnitude	tenure
multitude	torture
obstinacy	

Lesson 50 - States of Being

This lesson introduces the following suffixes:

ment - state of, quality of
ness - state of
tion, sion - state of, act of

Other Words with These Suffixes

abasement	oneness
achievement	opposition
alignment	participation
assumption	rejuvenate
business	restlessness
celebration	rudeness
clarification	sentiment
commitment	shabbiness
enlargement	syncopation
fleetness	tabulation
formation	tenderness
friendliness	tension
hesitation	torsion
limitation	unification
litigation	weariness

Lesson 51 - More States of Being

This lesson introduces the following suffixes:

ance, ancy - state of
ence, ency - state of
ity - state of
ship - state of

Other Words with These Suffixes

adversity	eternity
alliance	fraternity
ambiguity	frugality
amenity	hardship
assistance	hilarity
championship	irritability
clarity	militancy
conference	obedience
citizenship	patience
defiance	radiance
deficiency	resistance
dependency	tolerance
dignity	tranquility
dominance	urgency
endurance	vigilance
elegance	

Lesson 52 - People

This lesson introduces the following suffixes:

ar, er, or - one who
ist - one who

Other Words with These Suffixes

accompanyist	inquisitor
alarmist	jester
ambassador	juror
anarchist	liberator
arbiter	mariner
astrologer	miser
atheist	monitor
beggar	naturalist
chemist	optimist
competitor	orator
counselor	scholar
cyclist	scientist
donor	terrorist
editor	vendor
emperor	vocalist
evangelist	warrior
extremist	

Lesson 53 - in the Making

This lesson introduces the following suffixes:

ate - to make
en - to make
fy, ify - to make
ize - to make

Other Words with These Suffixes

animate	magnify
authorize	modify
brutalize	mutate
captivate	negate
cremate	negotiate
debate	radiate
delineate	ratify
dissipate	salivate
emphasize	satiate
energize	saturate
equalize	stiffen
familiarize	sympathize
fertilize	synchronize
fortify	tabulate
hasten	testify
harmonize	transmogrify
intonate	unify
irrigate	verify
itemize	weaken
liberate	whiten

Lesson 54 - Related To

This lesson introduces the following suffixes:

ary - related to
ery - related to
ory - related to

Other Words with These Suffixes

ancillary	incendiary
bravery	inflammatory
circulatory	mandatory
compensatory	necessary
contemporary	obligatory
contrary	planetary
corollary	predatory
defamatory	primary
dietary	stationery
evolutionary	voluntary
honorary	witchery

Word Study

Choose two vocabulary words and record information about each word on these cards.

Word _____

Definition _____

_____

Synonyms _____

Antonyms _____

Word Origin _____

Related Words (other forms or parts of speech) _____

_____

Word _____

Definition _____

_____

Synonyms _____

Antonyms _____

Word Origin _____

Related Words (other forms or parts of speech) _____

_____

Word Building Blocks

Fill in the chart with words that are derived from these prefixes and root words.

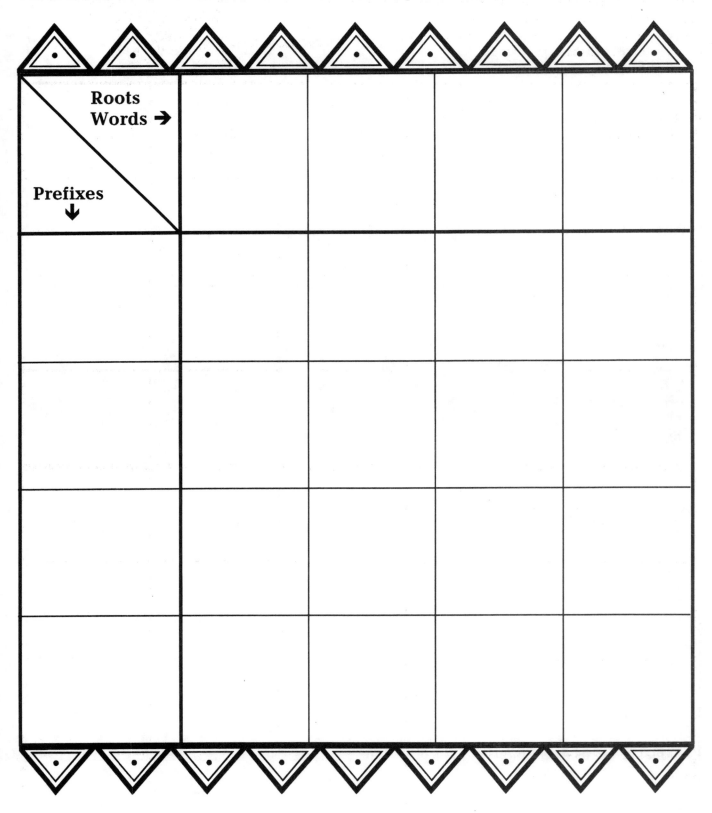

(Teachers - Choose the prefixes and root words you want to study. Write the prefixes along the right side and root words in the four spaces along the top. Have students combine the prefixes and root words and write the resultant words in the spaces where the two sections intersect.)

Parts of Speech

Choose three prefixes and three roots words. In the first column write the prefixes and root words and their meanings. In the following columns, record words for each part of speech that are derived from these word parts.

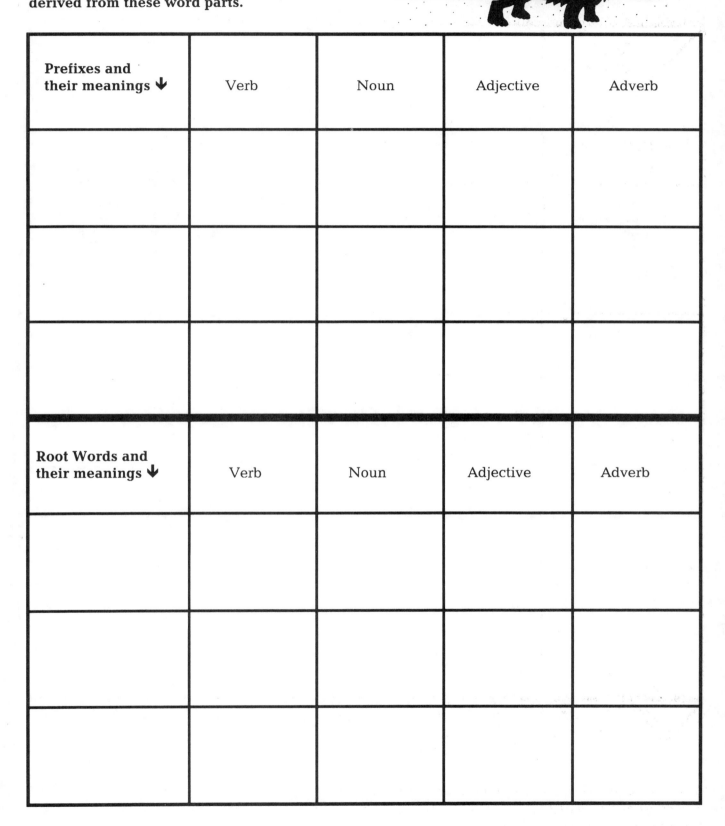

Prefixes and their meanings ↓	Verb	Noun	Adjective	Adverb

Root Words and their meanings ↓	Verb	Noun	Adjective	Adverb

Root Word Pyramid

Using the root word in the top box, find three words that are derived from this root. Write them in the next row of boxes. In the third row, write words that are related to the three words in the second row. In the boxes in the fourth row, write sentences for three of the words from the second or third row.

Root Word

Meaning

Three words from this root word

Another form of each of the three words in row two

Sentence   Sentence   Sentence

Word Quilt

Choose a prefix, suffix, or root word and write it in the center. In the four spaces that surround the center, write words that are formed from this word part. In the outside areas, write a definition for each of the four words.

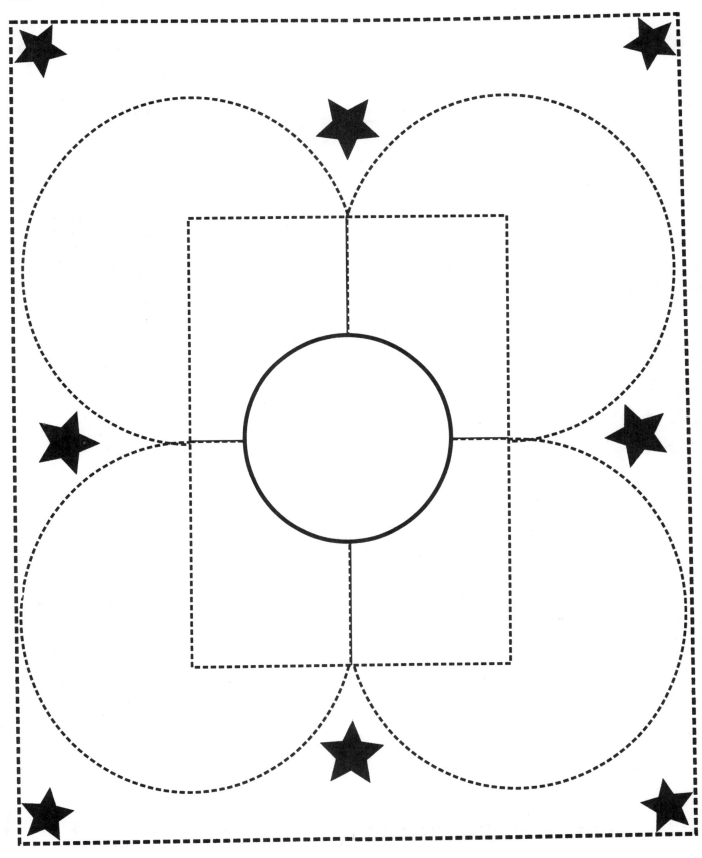

Worksheet Samples

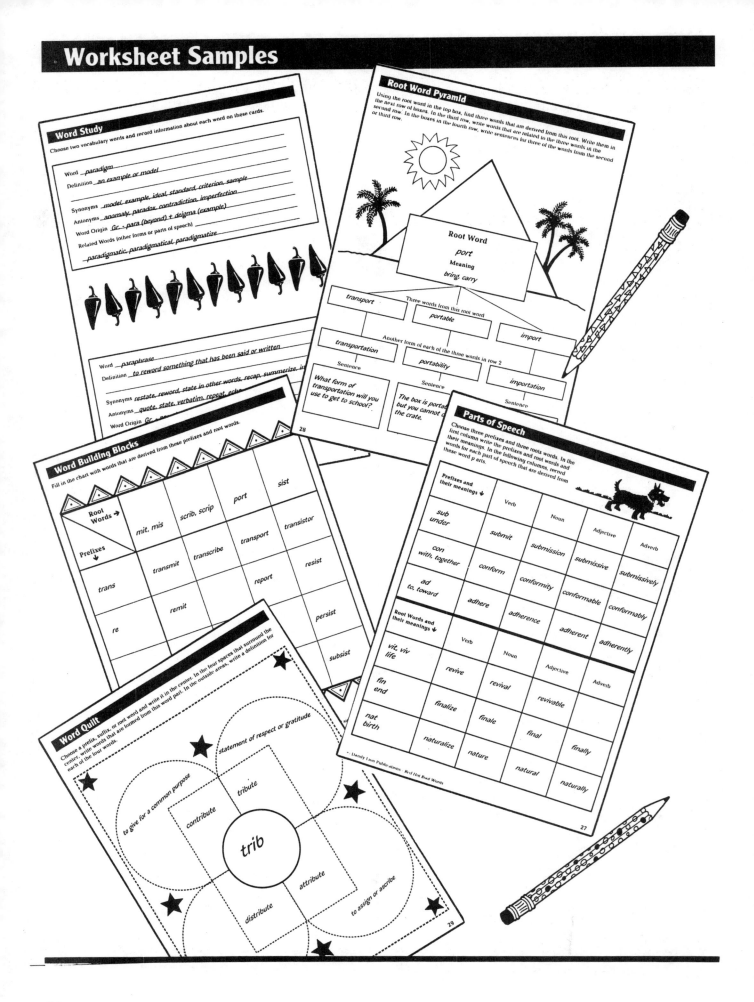

Word Study

Choose two vocabulary words and record information about each word on these cards.

Word _paradigm_
Definition _an example or model_

Synonyms _model, example, ideal, standard, criterion, sample_
Antonyms _anomaly, paradox, contradiction, imperfection_
Word Origin _Gr - para (beyond) + deigma (example)_
Related Words (other forms or parts of speech)
paradigmatic, paradigmatical, paradigmatize

Word _paraphrase_
Definition _to reword something that has been said or written_

Synonyms _restate, reword, state in other words, recap, summarize, in_
Antonyms _quote, state, verbatim, repeat, echo_
Word Origin _Gr -_

Root Word Pyramid

Using the root word in the top box, find three words that are derived from this root. Write them in the next row of boxes. In the third row, write words that are related to the three words in the second row. In the boxes in the fourth row, write sentences for three of the words from the second or third row.

Root Word
port
Meaning
bring, carry

Three words from this root word

transport
portable
import

Another form of each of the three words in row 2

transportation
portability
importation

Sentence
What form of transportation will you use to get to school?

Sentence
The box is porta[...] but you cannot [...] the crate.

Sentence

28

Word Building Blocks

Fill in the chart with words that are derived from these prefixes and root words.

Root Words →	mit, mis	scrib, scrip	port	sist
Prefixes ↓			transport	transistor
trans	transmit	transcribe	report	resist
re	remit			persist
				subsist

Parts of Speech

Choose three prefixes and three roots words. In the first column write the prefixes and root words and their meanings. In the following columns, record words for each part of speech that are derived from these word parts.

Prefixes and their meanings ↓	Verb	Noun	Adjective	Adverb
sub under	submit	submission	submissive	submissively
con with, together	conform	conformity	conformable	conformably
ad to, toward	adhere	adherence	adherent	adherently

Root Words and their meanings ↓	Verb	Noun	Adjective	Adverb
vit, viv life	revive	revival	revivable	
fin end	finalize	finale	final	finally
nat birth	naturalize	nature	natural	naturally

© Dandy Lion Publications Red Hot Root Words

27

Word Quilt

Choose a prefix, suffix, or root word and write it in the center. In the four spaces that surround the center, write words that are formed from this word part. In the outside areas, write a definition for each of the four words.

statement of respect or gratitude

to give for a common purpose

tribute

contribute

trib

attribute

distribute

to assign or ascribe

29

Over and Under

Prefixes	Meaning	Words You Already Know	
sub	*below, under*	**sub**marine	
trans	*across, over*	**trans**port	

New Words

Definitions	Sentences
subconscious (n) - the part of the mind's function of which you are not aware	*Something in my <u>subconscious</u> told me that things were not quite right.*
subdue (v) - to conquer or bring under control	*The lion tamer was able to <u>subdue</u> the agitated animal.*
subjugate (v) - to conquer or bring under control by force	*The military tried to <u>subjugate</u> the people who were rioting in the streets.*
subsidize (v) - to furnish money or to assist with the payment of money	*Her parents had to <u>subsidize</u> her expenses while she was in college.*
subterranean (adj) - beneath the earth's surface	*The <u>subterranean</u> cave took us down 500 meters from the cave's entrance.*
transcribe (v) - to make a written copy	*The executive asked her secretary to <u>transcribe</u> the notes from the meeting.*
transfer (v) - to carry or send from one person or place to another	*The unhappy student asked to be <u>transferred</u> to a different gym class.*
transform (v) - to change in form or appearance	*The fairy godmother <u>transformed</u> the pumpkin into a carriage.*
translucent (adj) - permitting some light to pass through but giving an unclear image	*The curtains were <u>translucent</u>, allowing only a little light to pass through.*
transplant (v) - to plant in another place	*I <u>transplanted</u> my entire flower garden to a spot where it could get more sun.*

Over and Under

Fill in the blanks in these sentences using vocabulary words.

1. Through the _____ curtain, I could see a vague outline of an old man.

2. The secretary _____ the notes for her boss.

3. Tear gas was used to _____ the rioting crowd.

4. I need to _____ a tree from my front yard to the back yard.

5. Mr. Yale went to the bank to _____ some money from his savings account to his checking account.

6. Parents should be prepared to _____ their children's college educations, because they usually can't make enough money to pay all of their expenses.

7. The warm water came from a _____ spring.

8. My _____ knew that it was not the right thing to do, even though my friend said it would be okay.

9. The dictator was determined to _____ all the people in the kingdom so he would have total control.

10. The magician _____ the rabbit into a chicken.

Here are some words that are not on your vocabulary list but use the same prefixes. Add the prefix *trans* or *sub* to these words and match them with their definitions.

11. _____ stitute ____   a. attempting to overthrow the government
12. _____ late ____   b. a deal or agreement
13. _____ versive ____   c. following
14. _____ action ____   d. to change from one language to another
15. _____ sequent ____   e. replacement

More, More, More

Prefixes	Meaning	Words You Already Know
hyper	*above, over, more*	**hyper**active
super, supr, sur	*above, over, more*	**super**ior, **supr**eme, **sur**face

New Words

Definitions	Sentences
hyperbole (n) - an intentional statement of exaggeration	*Her statement that she was so hungry that she could eat a cow was <u>hyperbole</u>.*
hypercritical (adj) - excessively critical	*His mother was <u>hypercritical</u>, always finding fault with his behavior.*
hypertension (n) - extreme tension; high blood pressure	*Speaking before an audience gives me <u>hypertension</u>.*
hyperthermia (n) - high temperature	*After two days of <u>hyperthermia</u>, he decided to see a doctor.*
superimpose (v) - lay one item atop another	*The magazine cover featured the picture of a bird <u>superimposed</u> over the image of the oil spill.*
superlative (adj) - of the highest order; best; greatest	*The king was the <u>superlative</u> ruler, more powerful than princes, dukes or lords.*
supernatural (adj) - beyond the laws of nature	*The movie featured many <u>supernatural</u> encounters that were scary.*
supervise (v) - oversee	*If you don't constantly <u>supervise</u> this dog, he will chew up everything in the room.*
surcharge (n) - additional charge or tax	*The city's <u>surcharge</u> on all hotel bills is called a bed tax.*
surplus (n) - more than what is needed	*Every year my dad has a <u>surplus</u> of zucchini and has to give it away to the neighbors.*

More, More, More

Find the one word in each line that means the same or most nearly the same as the first word.

1. **surplus**	materials	inadequate	abundance
2. **supervise**	direct	submit	children
3. **superlative**	increase	ultimate	least
4. **hyperbole**	de-emphasize	overstatement	discussion
5. **hypercritical**	praiseworthy	flattery	fault-finding
6. **surcharge**	tariff	taxable	money

Match each of the words below with a word that means the <u>opposite</u>.

7. ____ hypertension   a. understatement

8. ____ supernatural   b. separate

9. ____ superimpose   c. calm

10. ____ hyperbole   d. natural

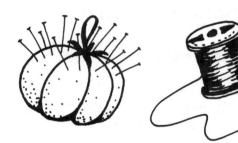

Fill in a word to complete each sentence.

11. The thermometer showed she had _____.

12. _____ the pattern over the fabric and then cut along the edge of the pattern.

13. The _____ on cigarette purchases was to be used for education.

14. He is a _____ swimmer; the best in his class.

15. Will you _____ the children while I run a short errand?

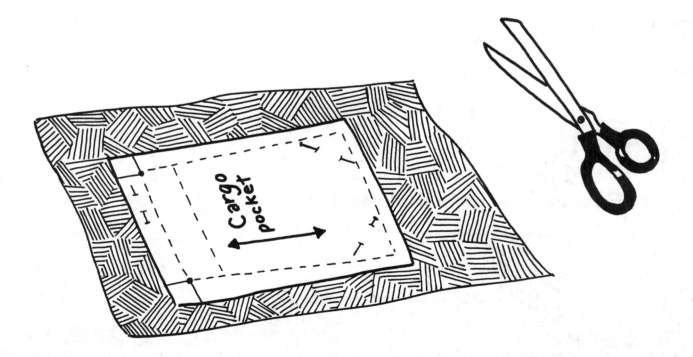

Before and After

Prefixes	Meaning	Words You Already Know	
fore	*before, toward*	**fore**see	Sincerely, Mary
pre	*before, toward*	**pre**pare	**P.S.** Dont' forget to feed the cat!
post	*after, behind*	**post**script	

New Words

Definitions	Sentences
forecast (v) - to predict or estimate in advance	*The weatherman <u>forecasted</u> that it will rain today.*
forethought (n) - a thought that comes beforehand, a prediction	*She had the <u>forethought</u> to bring along an umbrella in case it rained.*
forewarn (v) - to warn beforehand	*The weather bureau <u>forewarned</u> the residents of the approaching storm.*
posterior (n) - the back side	*The <u>posterior</u> of the house was plain, but the front was very attractive.*
posthumous (adj) - happening after someone's death	*The <u>posthumous</u> reading of his will offered many surprises about his wealth.*
postpone (v) - put off until a later time	*Would it be okay with you if we <u>postponed</u> our appointment until next week?*
preamble (n) - an introduction or introductory explanation	*The <u>preamble</u> briefly explained what the intent of the document was.*
precaution (n) - care taken beforehand	*Looking both ways before crossing the street is a <u>precaution</u> that everyone should practice.*
premature (adj) - happening or ripening before the natural or proper time	*The <u>premature</u> baby was born a month too soon and was very small.*
premier (n) - the first performance or showing	*The rock group's <u>premier</u> took place before a small but faithful group of fans.*

Before and After

For each sentence, find a vocabulary word to replace the underlined word or words.

1. Use <u>vigilance</u> so you don't get hurt on the hike. _____

2. If you had read the <u>introduction</u>, you would understand what the author is saying.

    _____

3. The crossing guard <u>alerted</u> the children of an approaching car. _____

4. She had the <u>farsightedness</u> to bring games for the children to play in the car. _____

5. His entrance on stage was <u>too early</u>, making everyone in the audience laugh. _____

6. The <u>rear</u> of the garden was filled with weeds. _____.

7. The band's <u>opening performance</u> was sold out months ahead of time. _____

This is a list of words from your vocabulary list and other words that use the same prefixes. Add *fore, pre,* **or** *post* **to each root word and match it to its meaning on the right.**

8. _____ humous ___   a. hinder

9. _____ cast ___   b. date afterward

10. _____ pone ___   c. predict

11. _____ mier ___   d. preconceived idea

12. _____ judice ___   e. after death

13. _____ warn ___   f. predecessor

14. _____ vent ___   g. opening performance

15. _____ date ___   h. caution

16. _____ runner ___   i. delay

Backward and Forward

Prefixes	Meaning	Words You Already Know
pro	*forward, before*	**pro**ceed
retro	*backwards*	**retro**fit

New Words

Definitions	Sentences
procrastinate (v) to put off doing something until a later time	*My brother <u>procrastinates</u> about doing the dishes so long that the water gets cold.*
profess (v) - to come forward and make a public declaration	*The politician <u>professed</u> to support education but voted against all funds for schools.*
prologue (n) - the introductory part of a book. play or poem	*The <u>prologue</u> often gives you information about why the author wrote the book.*
promontory (n) - the highest point of land projecting out over a body of water or land	*Standing on the <u>promontory</u>, you could see the entire valley below.*
propensity (n) - a natural inclination toward	*His <u>propensity</u> for making people laugh made him a popular teacher.*
retroactive (adj) - having an effect on things in the past	*The legislature passed a tax bill that was <u>retroactive</u> to six months ago.*
retrofire (v) - to ignite a retrorocket	*The rocket began to <u>retrofire</u> ten seconds after it lifted off the launch pad.*
retrogress (v) - move backward, especially to a earlier or worse state	*As the team continued to lose games, its standing <u>retrogressed</u> until it was in last place.*
retrospect (n) - looking back on the past	*In <u>retrospect</u>, I think I did the right thing.*
retrospective (adj) - looking back on the past or past events	*The museum's <u>retrospective</u> exhibit presented the last 50 years of technology.*

Backward and Forward

Choose the word or phrase that completes each sentence.

1. If you procrastinate, you _____ doing something. *(rush, delay, mismanage)*

2. The prologue of the book is like the _____. *(foreword, climax, index)*

3. A promontory is not a _____. *(hill, pinnacle, valley)*

4. When things are retroactive, they affect the _____. *(past, future, weather)*

5. To retrogress is to move _____. *(rapidly, forward, backward)*

6. His propensity for playing the piano was his _____. *(displeasure, talent, hobby)*

7. A retrospective art show would feature samples of _____ work. *(past, best, current)*

8. When you profess something, you _____. *(renounce privately, memorize entirely, declare publicly)*

9. The rocket's retrofire happened during _____. *(orbit, launch, landing)*

10. Retrospect is the same as _____ of the past. *(review, rejection, restoration)*

Complete this chart, filling in the correct prefix, root word, complete word, and/or meaning.

	Prefix	Root Word	Word	Meaning
11.	_____	fess	_____	declare
12.	retro	_____	_____	looking back
13.	pro	logue	_____	_____
14.	_____	_____	retroactive	_____
15.	pro	_____	propensity	_____

Around and Around

Prefixes	Meaning	Words You Already Know
cir, circum	*around*	**circum**ference
peri	*around, surrounding, near*	**peri**meter

New Words

Definitions	Sentences
circuit (n) - a revolving; a journey around; a route	*The delivery man's <u>circuit</u> took him to all parts of the city.*
circulatory (adj) - going in a circuit, circular	*The <u>circulatory</u> system includes the heart, veins, arteries, and capillaries.*
circumnavigate (v) - to sail around	*His attempt to <u>circumnavigate</u> the world in his small boat was ended by the large storm.*
circumstance (n) - the condition surrounding or related to an event	*He asked for a careful explanation of the <u>circumstances</u> of the accident.*
circumvent (v) - to go around or bypass	*It is better to face your problem straight on than try to <u>circumvent</u> it by blaming other people.*
period (n) - the interval between certain happenings	*The <u>period</u> between lunch and recess is two hours.*
periodic (adj) - happening at regular intervals; happening from time to time	*Her <u>periodic</u> trips to the dentist kept her teeth healthy and clean.*
perigee (n) - the point in the moon's or a satellite's orbit that is closest to the earth or body it is orbiting	*When the moon is at its <u>perigee</u>, does it appear larger than usual?*
periphery (n) - the outer boundary of something	*The <u>periphery</u> of the garden is surrounded by a small fence.*
periscope (n)- an instrument for seeing around things	*Using a <u>periscope</u>, he was able to spy on the animals on the other side of the fence.*

Around and Around

Match each word with the correct definition.

1. ___ circuit   a. bypass

2. ___ circumnavigate   b. reoccurring

3. ___ circumstance   c. route

4. ___ circumvent   d. interval

5. ___ period   e. border

6. ___ periodic   f. condition

7. ___ periphery   g. sail around

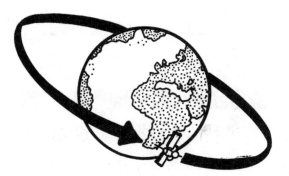

Complete these analogies.

8. _____ : seeing around :: telescope : seeing in the distance

9. perigee : _____ :: apogee : farthest

10. heart : _____ :: stomach : digestive

11. regular : _____ :: irregular : occasional

12. circumambulate : walking :: _____ : sailing

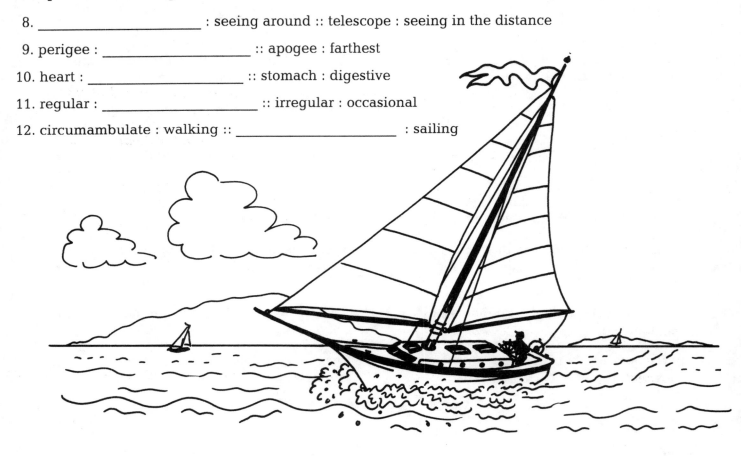

Finish the sentence by choosing the correct word.

13. To look around the corner of the building you would use a *(telescope, periscope, circuit)*.

14. A fence along the *(periphery, front, perigee)* of your yard would show where your property stops and the neighbor's property begins.

15. Water going down the drain flows in a *(gurgling, periodic, circulatory)* manner.

16. Exceptionally high ocean tides occur when the moon is at *(sunset, perigee, apogee)*.

Ways to Move

Prefixes	Meaning	Words You Already Know
ad	to, toward	**ad**vance
re	back, again	**re**peat
se	apart, away	**se**parate

New Words

Definitions	Sentences
adapt (v) - to change to be suitable or fit	If this type of frog can <u>adapt</u> to the pollution in the water, it may survive.
adhere (v) - to stick to something; conform to; obey	To make a bandage <u>adhere</u>, make sure you skin is dry when you put it on.
adjacent (adj) - close to, bordering on	The black car was parked <u>adjacent</u> to the red truck.
recurrent (adj) - happening again and again, returning periodically	A <u>recurrent</u> theme of his books is that bravery brings great rewards.
reimburse (v) - pay back, refund	I'll pay for your ticket to the theater if you <u>reimburse</u> me later.
reiterate (v) - repeat many times	Let me <u>reiterate</u> what I said so you won't forget.
secession (n) - the act of withdrawing from an alliance or association	The northern states threatened <u>secession</u> from the union if they didn't get more power in the government.
seclude (v) - to withdraw or set apart from social contact	The teacher <u>secluded</u> the talkative child by putting him in the corner by himself.
segregate (v) - to separate from the rest of the group	<u>Segregate</u> the geese from the ducks and put the ducks in the pen.
sequester (v) - to separate or withdraw; to choose solitude or retirement	After being around people all day, she just wanted to <u>sequester</u> herself in her bedroom.

Ways to Move

For each word on the right, choose the one word in the list of words that does <u>not</u> mean the same.

1. **adapt**	accommodate	abstract	adjust
2. **adhere**	obey	cling	detach
3. **recurrent**	unique	repetitious	repeated
4. **reiterate**	restate	whisper	repeat
5. **secession**	split away	defect	induct
6. **seclude**	include	separate	shut off
7. **segregate**	sequester	integrate	isolate
8. **sequester**	withdraw	hide	join in
9. **reimburse**	borrow	repay	remunerate
10. **adjacent**	next to	neighboring	diagonally

Choose the word that correctly completes the phrase or sentence.

11. Her _____ headaches were a source of irritation.
   a. receptive   b. adaptable   c. recurrent

12. The country's _____ puzzled the other countries left in the alliance.
   a. secession   b. adaptation   c. reimbursement

13. The store is located _____ to the library.
   a. attached   b. adjacent   c. adhesive

14. When animals cannot _____ to changes, they often become extinct.
   a. segregate   b. adopt   c. adapt

15. If you _____ the puppy, it will bark.
   a. secede   b. sedate   c. seclude

16. The teacher _____ the instructions for the test three times.
   a. refused   b. reiterated   c. secluded

Coming Through

Prefixes	Meaning	Words You already Know	
dia	*through, across*	**dia**meter, **dia**logue	
per	*through, across*	**per**ceive	

New Words

Definitions	Sentences
diagram (n) - a picture drawn to explain an idea	*On the test we had to draw a diagram to show how a circuit worked.*
diagnose (v) - to identify a disease through symptoms	*The doctor was quickly able to diagnose the child's disease as measles.*
diagonal (n) - a straight line through a figure from one corner to another corner	*The diagonal divided the square into two triangles.*
diaphanous (adj) - transparent, capable of being seen through	*The diaphanous top layer of material revealed a layer of darker material underneath.*
diaphragm (n) - a membrane that separates one thing from another, such as the chest cavity and the abdominal cavity	*When you breath, your diaphragm moves up and down, causing air to flow into and out of the lungs.*
perambulate (v) - to walk through, over or around	*The herd perambulated the area, crossing it several times in search of food.*
percolate (v) - to drip through a small opening or to filter a liquid	*Gradually the rain water percolated through the soil and into the underground cave.*
perforate (v) - to make holes in something	*If you perforate the convertible's roof, you're likely to have rain inside the car.*
persistence (n) - continuing stubbornly without giving up; determination	*His persistence finally paid off when he earned his black belt in karate.*
pervasive (adj) - having the power to be spread or to pass through	*The feeling of joy was pervasive, spreading throughout the celebrating group.*

Coming Through

Match each word with the correct definition on the right.

1. ____ diagram
2. ____ diagnose
3. ____ diagonal
4. ____ diaphanous
5. ____ diaphragm
6. ____ perambulate
7. ____ percolate
8. ____ perforate
9. ____ persistence
10. ____ pervasive

a. wander
b. diligence
c. identify
d. puncture
e. slanting line
f. far-reaching
g. sheer
h. membrane
i. depiction
j. leach

Add the prefixes _dia_ and _per_ to these root words. Write the complete word and a short definition.

11. _____ + gram (write) = _____ _____

12. _____ + gnos (know) = _____ _____

13. _____ + phane (shining) = _____ _____

14. _____ + sist (stand) = _____ _____

15. _____ + meter (measure) = _____ _____

16. _____ + lect (speak) _____ _____

44

Outside

Prefixes	Meaning	Words You Already Know
e, ec, ef, ex	out of, outside	emit, eclipse, effort, exit
extra, exter	out of, outside, excessive	extraterrestrial, exterior

New Words

Definitions	Sentences
eccentric (adj) - ignoring social conventions; odd	*The eccentric old man lived by himself and had strange habits but didn't hurt anyone.*
ecstasy (n) - happiness; overwhelming feelings of joy	*She experienced a feeling of ecstacy when it was announced that she was the winner.*
effervesce (v) - to give off bubbles; to show excitement or liveliness	*She seemed to effervesce and soon everyone was just as excited as she was.*
effusive - (adj) demonstrative; unreserved; overflowing; pouring out	*Her effusive personality made people doubt the sincerity of her compliments.*
eject (v) - throw out	*Because he was not wearing a seat belt, he was ejected from the car during the accident.*
emit (v) - to send out; discharge	*The beacon emitted a strong beam of light every 30 seconds.*
excerpt (n) - a selected passage from a book or article	*I enjoyed the excerpt so much that I now want to read the entire book.*
exodus (n) - a departure or journey away from a place	*The family's exodus from their homeland was dangerous and disheartening.*
expulsion (n) - a forcing out	*His bad behavior caused his expulsion from the organization.*
extrude (v) - force or press out	*The machine extruded the cereal in the shape of stars and moons.*

Outside

For each sentence find a vocabulary word to replace the underlined word or words.

1. _____ A steady stream of toothpaste was <u>thrust out</u> of the tube by the curious child.

2. _____ Try to contain your feelings of <u>elation</u>.

3. _____ The slow <u>retreat</u> of refugees took weeks to complete.

4. _____ All his neighbors thought he was <u>offbeat</u>.

5. _____ I didn't read the whole report, just a <u>portion</u>.

6. _____ She went on and on with <u>gushing</u> praise for her daughter.

7. _____ The old saying is, "Don't <u>throw out</u> the baby with the bath water."

8. _____ The soda <u>fizzed</u> when it was poured into the glass.

9. _____ After the tenants' <u>eviction</u>, the landlord thoroughly cleaned the house.

10. _____ The sewer <u>gave off</u> a foul smell.

Some of the words below are vocabulary words and some are other words that use the prefixes you are studying. Add one of the prefixes meaning *out of* or *outside* to each of these root words. Write the complete word and its meaning.

11. _____ + cent (center)   _____   _____

12. _____ + ject (throw)   _____   _____

13. _____ + puls (move)   _____   _____

14. _____ + ordinary (normal)   _____   _____

15. _____ + terr (land)   _____   _____

16. _____ + tend (stretch)   _____   _____

All Together

Prefixes	Meaning	Words You Already Know
co, col	*with, together*	**co**operate, **col**lect
com, con	*with, together*	**com**bine, **con**nect
syn, sym	*with, together*	**syn**onym, **sym**pathy

New Words

Definitions	Sentences
coexist (v) - to exist at the same time or in the same place	*The two tribes coexisted peacefully in the same area for about two hundred years.*
coherent (adj) - sticking together; connected, related in some way	*Her speech was coherent, each point following logically from the previous point.*
collaborate (v) - to labor together	*The scientists decided to collaborate in their research.*
collide (v) - to come together with great force; to clash	*The two football players collided with such force that they both ended up on the ground.*
composite (adj) - made of separate parts or elements	*Granite is a composite rock, made of basalt, quartz, and mica.*
compound (v) - bring together; (n) a mixture	*Steel is a compound made of iron and other metals.*
concordance (n) - an agreement or harmony	*The feuding countries reached a concordance that ended their disputes.*
congregate (v) - to gather together	*All the families in the neighborhood congregated for a potluck dinner.*
symmetry (n) - elements on both sides of a line that have the same shape, size and arrangement	*The design on the butterfly showed perfect symmetry.*
synthesize (v) - to form a new thing by combining parts from other things; to unite or merge	*The medical researcher synthesized a new drug by blending two existing remedies.*

All Together

Match each vocabulary word with the correct meaning in the left column.

1. ____ assemble
2. ____ crash together
3. ____ cooperate
4. ____ to create by merging
5. ____ exist together
6. ____ congruence
7. ____ connected
8. ____ mixture
9. ____ understanding
10. ____ made of separate parts

a. coexist
b. coherent
c. symmetry
d. collaborate
e. congregate
f. concordance
g. collide
h. composite
i. synthesize
j. compound

Choose the word that means the opposite of the word in bold.

11. **coherent**
   a. clear
   b. understandable
   c. disjointed

12. **composite**
   a. combined
   b. blended
   c. separated

13. **congregate**
   a. segregate
   b. meet
   c. gather

14. **symmetry**
   a. similarity
   b. asymmetry
   c. correspondence

15. **collaborate**
   a. counteract
   b. cooperate
   c. team up

16. **concordance**
   a. treaty
   b. truce
   c. disagreement

Moving Away

Prefixes	Meaning	Words You Already Know	
ab, abs	*away, from*	**ab**olish, **abs**ent	
apo	*away, from*	**apo**strophe, **apo**logy	**,**

New Words

Definitions	Sentences
abandon (v) - to leave or give up completely; to discontinue	*I am just going to <u>abandon</u> this science project and start an entirely new one.*
abdicate (v) - give up power, authority or the throne	*The king had to <u>abdicate</u> his throne and turn over power to his daughter, Princess Leah.*
abduct (v) - to take away by force, kidnap	*The men <u>abducted</u> the heiress and held her for a million dollar ransom.*
abnormal (adj) - not typical, average or normal	*Needing to sleep with a nightlight on each night is <u>abnormal</u> behavior for someone his age.*
aboriginal (n) - the original inhabitants of a country	*Though the <u>aboriginals</u> had lived in the area for generations, they owned very little property.*
absolute (adj) - without restraint, not dependent on anything	*His decision was <u>absolute</u>; there was no arguing with him.*
absolve (v) - to free from blame, debt or responsibility	*The kindly landlord <u>absolved</u> the poor tenant of all the past-due rent he owed.*
abstain (v) - to voluntarily refrain from	*I am trying to <u>abstain</u> from eating chocolate.*
abstract (adj) - not concrete or related to specific things; not easy to understand	*His lecture seemed very <u>abstract</u> and not related to real life.*
apogee (n) - the point in the moon's or a satellite's orbit when it is farthest from the earth or the body it orbits	*The opposite of the moon's <u>apogee</u> is its perigee.*

Moving Away

Read each statement and answer true or false.

1. **T   F**   Abstaining is something someone forces you to do.

2. **T   F**   Abnormal is the same as atypical.

3. **T   F**   If you abandon hope, you give up expectation.

4. **T   F**   When the moon is at its apogee, it is closest to the earth.

5. **T   F**   An abstract plan is clear and easy to follow.

6. **T   F**   Aboriginal is the same as native.

7. **T   F**   Abduct involves unwilling seizure.

8. **T   F**   To absolve someone is to carry a grudge forever.

9. **T   F**   The leader who abdicates his authority is left without power.

10. **T   F**   To give something your absolute support is to support it conditionally.

Use your vocabulary words to complete these sentences.

11. If you can't _____ from eating the jelly beans, maybe you should put them out of sight.

12. Picasso's paintings were _____ and mysterious.

13. The group of _____ were upset when their grave sites were disturbed.

14. _____ and _____ are two words that involve giving up.

15. The jury _____ the defendant of any guilt in the case.

Against

Prefixes	Meaning	Words You Already Know
ant, anti	*against*	**anti**freeze, **anti**septic
contra, counter	*against*	**counter**clockwise, **contra**st
ob	*against, facing*	**ob**serve, **ob**ject

New Words

Definitions	Sentences
antagonist (n) - an opponent	*The hero in the story was very kind, and the <u>antagonist</u> was extremely evil.*
antiseptic (n) - something used to kill germs; (adj) - free of germs	*She cleaned the wound with <u>antiseptic</u> before bandaging it.*
antisocial (adj) - unable to associate with other people; not sociable	*He's so <u>antisocial</u>; he never wants to do things with other people.*
contradiction (n) - a statement that is opposite to another statement	*Cory's statement was a <u>contradiction</u> of what James said happened.*
counterbalance (n) - a weight used to balance another weight; (v) - to balance or offset	*When sitting on a teeter totter, it's good to have someone about the same weight to <u>counterbalance</u> you.*
counterproductive (adj) - producing the opposite of what is desired or intended	*Her actions were completely <u>counterproductive</u>; in fact, they made the task more difficult.*
oblique (adj) - not straight; slanting, inclined, or sloping	*Draw an <u>oblique</u> line through the square to make two triangles.*
obnoxious (adj) - very unpleasant and objectionable	*The rotting fruit gave off an <u>obnoxious</u> smell.*
obscure (v) - to make unclear; to conceal or make less obvious	*He tried to <u>obscure</u> his footsteps by brushing a tree branch over the trail.*
obstinate (adj) - unyielding; unreasonably determined to have one's own way	*The <u>obstinate</u> child kicked and screamed when she didn't get what she wanted.*

© Dandy Lion Publications - *Red Hot Root Words*

51

Against

Add the correct prefix and select the meaning on the right.

1. _____ productive ___   a. enemy

2. _____ stinate ___   b. disagreement

3. _____ septic ___   c. slanting

4. _____ lique ___   d. unfriendly

5. _____ agonist ___   e. disguise

6. _____ noxious ___   f. stubborn

7. _____ scure ___   g. disinfectant

8. _____ balance ___   h. disgusting

9. _____ diction ___   i. not constructive

10. _____ social ___   j. equalized

Choose the vocabulary word that best fits in each sentence.

11. Though Charles rarely went to parties, he was not _____.
    (obnoxious   antisocial)

12. While he tried to help, his efforts were really _____ to what we were trying to accomplish.
    (counterbalance   counterproductive)

13. Don't be so _____. Give in just this one time.
    (obstinate   antisocial)

14. Her life was a _____. She always said one thing but acted very differently.
    (antagonist   contradiction)

15. The nurse used _____ ointment on the cut.
    (antiseptic   oblique)

16. The younger child drew _____ lines, while the older child drew horizontal ones.
    (oblique   obnoxious)

Numbers 1-4

Prefixes	Meaning	Words You Already Know
mono, uni	*one*	**mono**cle, **uni**t
bi, du	*two*	**du**et, **bi**cycle
tri	*three*	**tri**angle
quad, quar	*four*	**quad**ruple, **quar**ter

New Words

Definitions	Sentences
monochrome (adj) - one color	*The blue, <u>monochrome</u> painting was boring.*
monopoly (n) - control by one person or one company	*Thomas Rich had a <u>monopoly</u> on all the real estate in the center of the city.*
unicorn (n) - a horse-like animal with one horn	*The fairy tale featured a young princess and her pet <u>unicorn</u>.*
unify (v) - to make one	*The king tried to <u>unify</u> all the small serfdoms into one strong kingdom.*
duplex (n) - a house that has two separate units	*Jorge lived in one of the <u>duplexes</u> and his friend Bryan lived next door.*
biennial (adj) - happening every two years	*The <u>biennial</u> celebration took place in even-numbered years.*
bilingual (adj) - speaking two languages	*Many people in Quebec are <u>bilingual</u>, speaking both English and French.*
trilogy (n) - a group of three plays or books with a common theme	*I have read all three books in the <u>trilogy</u>, but I like the first book best.*
triathlon (n) - an athletic contest usually involving swimming, running and biking	*She completed all three events in the <u>triathlon</u> in record time, winning the contest.*
quadrangle (n) - a figure with four sides and angles	*Squares and rectangles are examples of <u>quadrangles</u>.*

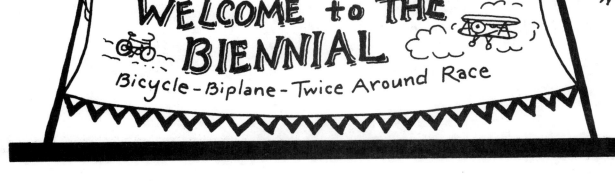

Numbers 1 - 4

Match each word with its meaning. Add one more word and its meaning to each group.

1. ____ unify
2. ____ monologue
3. ____ monopoly
4. ____ unilateral
5. ____ monochrome
6. ____ unicorn
7. _____

a. one-person show
b. one-horned animal
c. bring together
d. one color
e. one-sided
f. exclusive power

8. ____ duplex
9. ____ bifocal
10. ____ bilingual
11. ____ duet
12. ____ biennial
13. ____ duplicate
14. _____

a. every two years
b. make twofold
c. house or apartment with two units
d. music performed by two people
e. speaking two languages
f. two lenses

15. ____ trilogy
16. ____ triplets
17. ____ triathlon
18. ____ triangle
19. _____

a. sporting competition with three events
b. figure with three angles and sides
c. three books
d. three children born at the same time

20. ____ quadrangle
21. ____ quartet
22. ____ quadrant
23. ____ quarterly
24. _____

a. fourth of a circle
b. issued four times a year
c. figure with four angles and sides
d. music group with four people

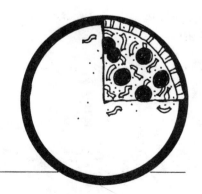

Numbers 5 - 10

Prefixes	Meaning	Words You Already Know
penta, quint	*five*	**penta**gon, **quint**et
sex, hexa	*six*	**sex**tuplet
sept, septem	*seven*	**Sept**ember
oct, octo	*eight*	**oct**opus, **Oct**ober
nov, non	*nine*	**Nov**ember, **noon**
dec, deci, deca	*ten*	**deci**mal, **Dec**ember

New Words

Definitions	Sentences
quintuplet (n) - one of five offspring born at the same time	*The babysitter found it confusing to remember the five <u>quintuplets'</u> names.*
pentagram - (n) - any figure made of five lines	*The teacher drew a star-shaped <u>pentagram</u> on all the papers with perfect scores.*
hexagon - (n) - a figure with six sides	*The store's sign was a <u>hexagon</u> with each of the six sides painted a different color.*
sextant - (n) a sixth of a circle; an instrument for measuring angles	*Sailing ships used to always have a <u>sextant</u> on board to help determine their positions.*
septennial (adj) - lasting seven years; happening every seven years	*There are very few <u>septennial</u> reunions, as most are celebrated every five or ten years, not seven.*
octagon (n) - a figure with eight sides	*A stop sign is in the shape of an <u>octagon</u>.*
octave (n) - a group of eight lines; eight notes; any group of eight	*You play this melody on the piano, and I will play the same tune one <u>octave</u> higher.*
decade (n) - ten years	*There was a difference of exactly three <u>decades</u> between Robert's age and his father's age.*
decathlon (n) - a contest with ten different events	*It takes great skill and stamina to take part in a <u>decathlon</u>.*
decimeter (n) - one tenth of a meter	*Using a meter stick, he measured the width of the piece of paper and found it was two <u>decimeters</u>.*

Numbers 5 - 10

Write a word for each definition. Add one more word for each number.

1. five offspring _____

2. figure made with five lines _____

3. _____ _____

4. six-sided figure _____

5. sixth of a circle _____

6. _____ _____

7. lasting seven years _____

8. _____ _____

9. figure with eight sides _____

10. group of eight _____

11. _____ _____

12. ten years _____

13. contest with ten events _____

14. one tenth of a meter _____

15. _____ _____

Beside, Between and Among

Prefixes	Meaning	Words You Already Know
epi	*on, beside, among*	**epi**sode
inter	*between, among*	**inter**fere, **inter**section
para	*beside, beyond*	**para**graph, **para**llelogram

New Words

Definitions	Sentences
epidemic (n) - a disease that spreads in a certain area; (adj)- spreading rapidly	*After the flood an epidemic of typhoid fever spread through the area.*
epidermis (n) - the outer layer of skin	*The injury was not very deep; it just cut the epidermis.*
epilogue (n) - a speech at the end of a play or the concluding part of a story	*In the epilogue the heroine is reunited with her family.*
intercede (v) - to act between two parties to restore peace; to mediate	*The teacher had to intercede in the playground dispute between the two groups.*
interim (n) - a period of time between two events; meantime	*The interim between when we hooked the fish and were able to land it seemed like an eternity.*
parable (n) - a simple story from which a moral can be drawn	*The moral of the parable is, "slow and steady wins the race."*
paradigm (n) - an example or model	*Her report became the paradigm for all other students to follow.*
parallel (adj) - at the same distance apart at every point; never meeting	*The two rails on the railroad track are parallel.*
paralysis (n) - a loss of sensation and the ability to move	*The skiing accident resulted in paralysis of both his legs.*
paraphrase (v) - to reword a statement	*Don't copy all the information, just paraphrase what it says.*

Beside, Between and Among

Circle the word that <u>does not</u> mean the same as the first word.

1. **epidemic**	plague	curse	pestilence
2. **epidermis**	fingernail	skin	cuticle
3. **epilogue**	postscript	conclusion	prologue
4. **intercede**	mediate	intervene	interrupt
5. **interim**	meantime	immediately	interlude
6. **parable**	novel	allegory	fable
7. **paradigm**	example	exception	standard
8. **parallel**	equispaced	side by side	intersecting
9. **paralysis**	locomotion	immobility	crippling
10. **paraphrase**	restate	contradict	summarize

Write the correct vocabulary word in each sentence.

11. Don't read it exactly, just _____ it.

12. Her enthusiasm was _____, affecting every one in the room.

13. His academic record was a _____ for all his younger brothers, who tried to get as good grades.

14. I didn't understand the neighbor's role in the novel until it was explained in the _____.

15. The moral of the _____ is, "Don't worry about what you can't control."

16. You could _____ or you could just mind your own business.

Down and Away

Prefixes	Meaning	Words You Already Know
cata	*down, away from*	**cata**pult
de	*down, away from*	**de**cline, **de**crease
tele	*far, distance*	**tele**phone

New Words

Definitions	Sentences
catacomb (n) - underground cave or tomb	*In the <u>catacomb</u> the archeologists found mummies that were thousands of years old.*
catalyst (n) - a substance that speeds up or causes a reaction; something that causes activity between two or more people	*Once the chemist put the <u>catalyst</u> in the mixture, it quickly turned into a solid mass.*
catastrophe (n) - tragic event; sudden disaster or misfortune	*The traffic accident was a <u>catastrophe</u> that affected several families.*
debark (v) - to exit a ship; to go on land	*We were scheduled to <u>debark</u> the cruise ship in Stockholm at 4 o'clock.*
default (v) - failure to do something, be somewhere, or pay money that is due	*Because they <u>defaulted</u> on their house loan, they found it difficult to get any other loans.*
degrade (v) - to lower in status; to show contempt or dishonor	*Mary's comments were critical of the committee's chairwoman and <u>degraded</u> her status among other members.*
depose (v) - to remove from office	*After the revolution the king was <u>deposed</u> and replaced by the leader of the military.*
telemarket (v) to sell products or services over the telephone	*One way to sell our product is to target people who would buy it and <u>telemarket</u> directly to them.*
telepathy - (n) - communication by means other than normal sensory communication	*The psychic said she could communicate with people via <u>telepathy</u>.*
telephoto - (adj) - a camera lens that makes distant objects appear closer	*The camera's <u>telephoto</u> lense allowed me to take a picture of a bear from a safe distance.*

Down and Away

Use a vocabulary word to correctly complete each sentence.

1. The ability to communicate without words is _____.

2. To fail to repay a loan is to _____ on the loan.

3. An underground tomb is a _____.

4. To dethrone a king is the same as to _____ him.

5. You _____ the meaning of our nation's flag when you use it for a curtain.

6. To sell things by telephone is to _____.

7. You could call it a tragedy or a _____.

8. Her input acted as a _____ for the conversation.

9. You exit a room and you _____ a ship.

10. For long-distance shots, use a _____ lens.

Add a prefix (cata, de, tele) to the last part of the words and then match the complete word with its meaning.

11. _____ strophe   a. dishonor

12. _____ grade   b. extrasensory perception

13. _____ pult   c. go down in value

14. _____ pathy   d. send pictures over a distance

15. _____ preciate   e. a calamity

16. _____ vise   f. launch or hurl

© Dandy Lion Publications - *Red Hot Root Words*

In and Into

Prefixes	Meaning	Words You Already Know	
en, em	*in, into, with*	**en**liven, **em**ploy	
in, im	*in*	**in**hale, **im**port	
intro, intra	*in, into*	**intro**duce, **intra**mural	

New Words

Definitions	Sentences
embellish (v) - add detail to make more beautiful; to decorate or add ornamentation	*The bride's dress was <u>embellished</u> with pearls and lace.*
embody (v) - to give bodily form to; to give tangible or concrete form to	*Her life <u>embodied</u> the principals of love, patience and forgiveness.*
enamor (v) - to be in love with; to charm; to captivate	*The librarian was <u>enamored</u> of books.*
imbibe (v) - to consume a liquid; to absorb; to drink in; to take into the mind	*His habit of <u>imbibing</u> ten sodas a day was not good for his health.*
immigrate (v) - to come to a country different from one's native country	*My ancestors <u>immigrated</u> to this country 100 years ago from Norway.*
induct (v) - bring into a group as a member	*The club <u>inducts</u> new members at the first meeting of each month.*
influx (n) - a flowing in; a continuous stream of people or things	*There was a sudden <u>influx</u> of water in the stream when the dam developed a leak.*
intrastate (adj) - occurring within a state	*All <u>intrastate</u> roads are maintained by the state highways department.*
introspection (n) - looking within; an analysis of one's own mental and emotional state	*After some <u>introspection</u>, I realize that I was terribly wrong.*
introvert (v) - to focus all interests and emotions on oneself; to turn inward	*Charles would be happier if he would share his feelings instead of <u>introverting</u> them.*

In and Into

Tell whether the two words in each pair have the same or different meanings.

1. embellish – adorn   same   different
2. embody – extrasensory   same   different
3. enamor – enrapture   same   different
4. imbibe – abstain   same   different
5. immigrate – emigrate   same   different
6. induct – install   same   different
7. influx – effluent   same   different
8. intrastate – interstate   same   different
9. introspection – self-examination   same   different
10. introvert – extrovert   same   different

Use vocabulary words to complete these sentences.

11 This trucking company only ships _____; it does not deliver to other states.

12. The fund-raiser had a last-minute _____ of money.

13. Using the glue gun, I was able to quickly _____ the picture frame with small decorations.

14. Our hiking group _____ed three new members.

15. Hillary used her journal writing for _____ and also to record important happenings in her life.

© Dandy Lion Publications - *Red Hot Root Words*

The Size of Things

Prefixes	Meaning	Words You Already Know
mega	*large, great*	**mega**phone
multi	*many*	**multi**ply, **multi**vitamin
poly	*many*	**poly**gon
semi, hemi	*half*	**semi**circle

New Words

Definitions	Sentences
hemisphere (n) - half of the world or globe	*Canada is in the northern <u>hemisphere</u>, and Australia is in the southern <u>hemisphere</u>.*
megalith (n) - a large prehistoric stone monument	*Stonehenge consists of several <u>megaliths</u> arranged in a circle.*
megalopolis (n) - very large city or urban area	*The <u>megalopolis</u> has a lot of problems that you don't find in a smaller city.*
multifaceted (adj) - having many facets, as in precious stones; having many talents	*Leonardo da Vinci, with his many talents, was the ultimate <u>multifaceted</u> person.*
multinational (adj) - having interests in many foreign countries; many nations	*The <u>multinational</u> force moved in to help bring peace to the region.*
multitude (n) - a great number of people or things; a crowd	*The <u>multitude</u> moved slowly and patiently through the ticket gate.*
polychromatic (adj) - having many colors	*The colorful quilt was <u>polychromatic</u>.*
polytheistic (adj) - the belief in more than one religion or gods	*The ancient Greeks and Egyptians had <u>polytheistic</u> religions with gods and goddesses for different forces in nature.*
semimonthly (adj) - something happening twice a month	*The baseball club met <u>semimonthly</u> on the first and third Monday.*
semitransparent (adj) - partially allowing light to pass through	*Only a small amount of light came through the <u>semitransparent</u> glass.*

The Size of Things

Read each statement and decide whether it is true or false.

1. **T F** A gathering of three people is not a multitude.

2. **T F** Monotheistic and polytheistic mean the same.

3. **T F** Semitransparent is the same as diaphanous.

4. **T F** The Earth's northern hemisphere is everything north of the equator.

5. **T F** Polychromatic involves many languages.

6. **T F** Multinational refers to more than one nation.

7. **T F** A megalopolis is a quiet, peaceful place to live.

8. **T F** A cut diamond is multifaceted.

9. **T F** If you make semimonthly payments, that's the same as making payments bimonthly.

10. **T F** A megalith is large and old.

Write the vocabulary words with the following meanings.

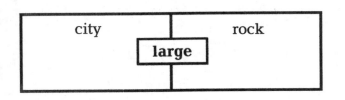

city		rock
	large	

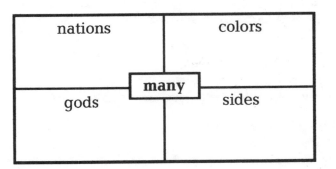

nations		colors
gods	**many**	sides

Just Not

Prefixes	Meaning	Words You Already Know
a, an	*not*	**an**tonym
il, ir	*not*	**il**legal, **ir**regular
im, in	*not*	**im**possible, **in**ability,
non	*not*	**non**sense

New Words

Definitions	Sentences
anonymous (adj) - without a name or with an unknown name	*I don't know who wrote the book because the author was <u>anonymous</u>.*
atypical (adj) - not typical, abnormal	*Riding a skateboard is <u>atypical</u> behavior for a cat.*
illiterate (adj) - unable to read or write	*Because he was <u>illiterate</u>, it was difficult for him to get a decent-paying job.*
illogical (adj) - not logical, unsound	*She did not convince me with her <u>illogical</u> argument.*
improbable (adj) - unlikely to happen	*Having a comet land in your back yard is possible but very <u>improbable</u>.*
inanimate (adj) - dead; not living	*The rocks in his collection were <u>inanimate</u>, but the reptiles were living.*
inclement (adj) - stormy; not kind or nice	*The <u>inclement</u> weather meant that the class could not go on its planned picnic.*
irrepressible (adj) - not able to be kept under control	*The toddler's energy was <u>irrepressible</u>, and her parents had a hard time controlling her.*
nonentity (n) - a person or thing that is of little importance	*The new student sat sadly in the back of the room, feeling like a <u>nonentity</u>.*
nonsensical (adj) - not making sense	*The singer sang a <u>nonsensical</u> tune about a frog with a college education.*

Just Not

Choose the word in each line that means the same or nearly the same as the first word.

1. **anonymous**	infamous	unnamed	pseudonym
2. **atypical**	abnormal	ordinary	commonplace
3. **illiterate**	scholarly	ill-mannered	uneducated
4. **illogical**	rational	sensible	unreasonable
5. **improbable**	unlikely	predictable	improper
6. **inanimate**	animation	lifeless	inane
7. **inclement**	blustery	weather	mild
8. **irrepressible**	irresistible	restrained	uncontrollable
9. **nonentity**	nothing	dignitary	nobility
10. **nonsensical**	thoughtful	ridiculous	conventional

Write a vocabulary word in each of the outside sections of the circle that matches the definition in the two inner sections.

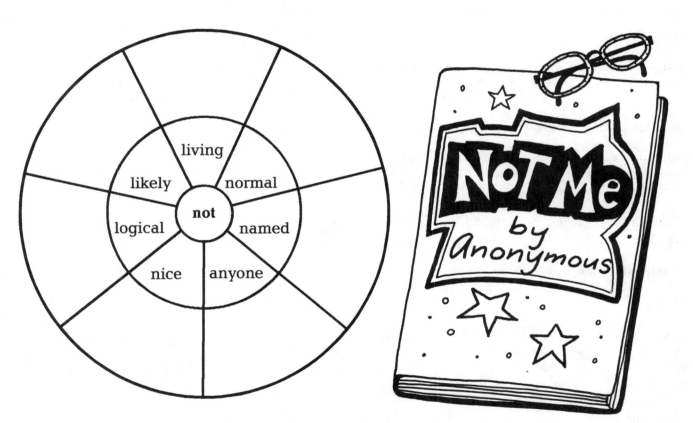

Listing of Prefixes

Prefixes	Meaning	Sample Words
a, an	*not*	See Lesson 18
ab, abs	*away, from*	See Lesson 10
ad	*to, toward*	See Lesson 6
ambi, amphi	*both*	ambiguous, ambidextrous, ambition, ambivalence, ambivalent, amphibian, amphitheater, amphora
ant, anti	*against*	See Lesson 11
ante	*before*	antebellum, antecedent, anterior, anticipate
apo	*away, from*	See Lesson 10
arch	*first*	archetype, architect, archbishop
bene	*good, well*	beneficial, benevolent, benefactor, benediction, beneficiary, benefit
bi	*two*	See Lesson 12
bon	*good*	bonus, bonanza, bona fide
cata	*down, away from*	See Lesson 15
cent	*hundred*	century, centipede, centennial
cir, circum	*around*	See Lesson 5
co, col	*with, together*	See Lesson 9
com, con	*with, together*	See Lesson 9
contra, counter	*against*	See Lesson 11
de	*down, away from*	See Lesson 15
dec, deci, deca	*ten*	See Lesson 13
demi	*half*	demitasse, demigod
dia	*through, across*	See Lesson 7
du	*two*	See Lesson 12
e, ec, ef, ex	*out of, outside*	See Lesson 8
en, em	*in, into, with*	See Lesson 16
epi	*on, beside, among*	See Lesson 14

Prefixes	Meaning	Sample Words
equi	*equal*	equidistant, equitable, equator, equivalent, equilateral, equilibrium, equity, equivocate
eu	*good*	eureka, eulogy, euphonious, euphoria, euphemism, euphonic, euphoric,
extra, exter	*outside, excessive*	See Lesson 8
for	*against, away*	forbid, forsake, forswear, forbear, forgo
fore	*before, toward*	See Lesson 3
hemi	*half*	See lesson 17
heter	*different*	heterogeneous, heterochromatic, heteronym heterosexual
hexa	*six*	See Lesson 13
holo	*whole*	holocaust, hologram, holography, holistic
hom, homo	*same*	homogeneous, homonym, homograph homogeny, homogenize
hyp, hypo	*under*	hypocrisy, hypothermia, hypothesis, hypothetical
hyper	*above, over, more*	See Lesson 2
il, ir	*not*	See Lesson 18
im, in	*in, into*	See Lesson 16
im, in	*not*	See Lesson 18
inter	*between, among*	See Lesson 14
intra, intro	*in, into*	See Lesson 16
kilo	*thousand*	kilogram, kilometer, kilowatt
mal, male	*bad*	malicious, malevolent, malformed, malignant, malcontent, malaise, malefactor, maleficent, malfunction, malice, malnutrition, maladjusted, malapropism, malignant, malodorous, malady, malicious
medi	*middle*	median, medieval, mediocre, media Mediterranean, mediate, medium
med	*half, between*	immediate, medial, mediate, mediation
mega	*large, great*	See Lesson 17
meta	*change, after, beyond*	metamorphosis, metaphor, metabolism, metaphysics

Prefixes	Meaning	Sample Words
mill	*thousand*	millipede, millennium, millimeter, million, milligram, millionaire
mono	*one*	See Lesson 12
multi	*many*	See Lesson 17
neo	*new*	neophyte, neologism, neonatal, neoimpressionism, neoprene
non	*not*	See Lesson 18
non, nov	*nine*	See Lesson 13
ob	*against, facing*	See Lesson 11
oct, octo	*eight*	See Lesson 13
of	*against*	offend, offensive
omni	*all*	omnivore, omnibus, omnipresent, omniscient, omnipotent
ortho	*straight, right*	orthodontics, orthopedic, orthodox, orthography
pan	*all*	panorama, panacea, pandemonium, panchromatic, pandemic, panoply
para	*beside, beyond*	See Lesson 14
penta	*five*	See Lesson 13
per	*through, across*	See Lesson 7
peri	*around, surrounding*	See Lesson 5
plu	*more*	plus, plural, plurality, plutocracy
poly	*many*	See Lesson 17
post	*after, behind*	See Lesson 3
pre	*before, toward*	See Lesson 3
pro	*before, forward*	See Lesson 4
proto	*first*	prototype, proton, protozoa, protocol, protoplasm, protoplast
quad, quar	*four*	See Lesson 12
quint	*five*	See Lesson 13
re	*back, again*	See Lesson 6
retro	*backwards*	See Lesson 4
sat	*enough*	satisfy, saturate, satiable, satisfactory, satiate, satiety, satire

Prefixes	Meaning	Sample Words
se	*back, again*	See Lesson 6
semi	*half*	See Lesson 17
sept, septem	*seven*	See Lesson 13
sex	*six*	See Lesson 13
sub	*below, under*	See Lesson 1
sur, super, supr	*above, over, more*	See Lesson 2
sym, syn	*with, together*	See Lesson 9
tele	*far, distance*	See Lesson 15
trans	*across, over*	See Lesson 1
tri	*three*	See Lesson 12
ulti	*last*	ultimate, ultima, ultimatum
ultra	*excessive*	ultramarine, ultrasonic, ultramodern, ultraviolet
un	*not*	unknown, unassailable, unconventional, unadorned, unabridged, unequivocal
uni	*one*	See Lesson 12
well	*good*	welcome, well-read, well-behaved, well-done, well-wisher

Bringing and Building

Root Words	Meaning	Words You Already Know
port	bring, carry	transport
struct, stru	build	construct

New Words

Definitions	Sentences
construe (v) - to explain, translate, or assume the meaning of something	*Don't construe what he said to mean that he liked the show.*
deport (v) - to send out of the country (usually a person)	*The man was deported to his native country by the immigration officials.*
deportee (n) - someone who is sent out of the country	*The deportee was not happy about returning to his native country.*
destructive (adj) - causing something to be destroyed or demolished	*The fire was very destructive, causing a million dollars' worth of damage.*
export (v) - to send goods out of one country to another country for the purpose of selling	*The company's business doubled once it started exporting its products to other countries.*
import (v) - to bring goods from a foreign country into a country for the purpose of selling	*There are many products we import because we cannot grow them in our country.*
instrumental (adj) - helpful; useful	*She was instrumental in getting an agreement among all the companies.*
obstruct (v) - to block or put obstacles in the way	*The guard tried to obstruct the center's attempt to make a basket.*
portable (adj) - capable of being carried	*He took his portable CD player with him to the beach.*
structural (adj) - related to building or construction	*The earthquake caused structural damage, but no people were hurt.*

Bringing and Building

Tell whether the two words in each pair have the same or different meanings.

1. construe — interpret   same   different
2. exile — deport   same   different
3. deportee — immigrant   same   different
4. beneficial — destructive   same   different
5. export — import   same   different
6. instrumental — assisting   same   different
7. obstruct — unblock   same   different
8. portable — immovable   same   different

Write a meaning for each of the following words.

9. porter (port + er) _____

10. reconstruct (re + construct) _____

11. infrastructure (infra + structure) _____

Write a brief, but complete answer for each question. Write your answers on the back of this paper or on another sheet of paper.

12. Name three things in the room that are <u>portable</u>.

13. Describe a time when you were <u>instrumental</u>.

14. Describe a time when you tried to <u>obstruct</u> someone or something.

15. Describe one <u>structural</u> feature of your school.

16. Make a diagram that shows the difference between <u>import</u> and <u>export</u>.

Ways of Writing

Root Words	Meaning	Words You already Know
graph, gram	write, writing	autograph, telegram
scrip, scrib	write, writing	script, scribble

New Words

Definitions	Sentences
autobiography (n) - an account of one's own life	His <u>autobiography</u> told only about the complimentary parts of his life.
calligraphy (n) - beautiful, fancy writing	She practiced her <u>calligraphy</u> until she could make each letter perfectly.
conscript (v) - to force into service or labor for government	The government <u>conscripted</u> all men between the ages of 18 and 25 to be in the army.
epigram (n) - a short, witty poem; a witty, clever saying	His speech was spiced with <u>epigrams</u> that kept the audience entertained.
geography (n) - science dealing with the earth's surface and its features	The <u>geography</u> of the area included mountains, plateaus, and valleys.
graphic (adj) - providing a clear picture; vivid and realistic; written or drawn	The author's <u>graphic</u> description of the setting made you feel like you were really there.
inscription (n) - something that is written or engraved, especially on a solid surface	The <u>inscription</u> on the gravestone was barely readable because it was so old.
monograph (n) - a book or article about a single subject	The scientist's <u>monograph</u> covers his research on cell division.
prescription (n) - an order or direction; a doctor's instructions for the use of medicine	The <u>prescription</u> said to take the medication three times a day.
transcript (n) - a written or typewritten copy	The executive asked her secretary to make a <u>transcript</u> of the notes of the meeting.

Ways of Writing

For each sentence find the vocabulary word that means the same or nearly the same as the underlined words.

1. Her gift was a poem that was written in <u>beautiful script</u> and framed. _____

2. During the war the soldier was <u>forced into doing labor</u> for the enemy. _____

3. The anthropologist's latest <u>book about one topic</u> was unusual. Usually he wrote textbooks about many topics. _____

4. The doctor wrote an <u>order</u> for the patient to take antibiotics for the infection. _____

5. After her acting career slowed down, the actress wrote <u>an account of her life</u>. _____

6. The lawyer provided the judge with <u>a written copy</u> of the evidence she would be presenting in the trial. _____

7. The class made rubbings of the <u>engraved messages</u> on the tombs in the graveyard. _____

8. One of the comedian's talents was the ability to quickly come up with <u>clever comments</u> about almost any situation. _____

9. The newspaper's account of the crime scene was very <u>vivid</u>. _____

10. The test on the <u>earth's features</u> included drawing and labeling all the major mountain chains in the country. _____

Answer each question true or false.

11. **T F**   If you write a monograph, you write about only one subject.

12. **T F**   An autobiography is a book about cars.

13. **T F**   A prescription is the same as a subscription.

14. **T F**   If you are skilled at calligraphy, you have perfected your penmanship.

15. **T F**   If you study geography, you study mountains, rivers, valleys, and other land features.

Reaching the End

Root Words	Meaning	Words You Already Know	
fin	*end*	**fin**ish	
sat	*enough*	**sat**isfy	
term	*end*	**term**inal	

New Words

Definitions	Sentences
confine (v) - to keep within certain limits; to imprison	*It was hard to <u>confine</u> the toddler to one area of the house.*
definitive (adj) - final; most accurate and complete	*Her <u>definitive</u> answer was that I could not go bungee jumping.*
determine (v) - to set limits, to define	*The principal will have to <u>determine</u> the best way to handle the problem.*
finale (n) - the last scene of a show or the last movement of a musical performance	*For the <u>finale</u> the orchestra played a concerto by Mozart.*
indeterminable (adj) - cannot be determined or decided	*The damage from the hurricane is <u>indeterminable</u> at this point.*
infinite (adj) - without limits; endless	*Looking up at the night sky, it seemed like there were an <u>infinite</u> number of stars.*
insatiable (adj) - unable to satisfy; greedy	*My need to eat chocolate is sometimes <u>insatiable</u>.*
saturate (v) - to soak thoroughly; to fill fully	*The rain <u>saturated</u> her clothes so she had to change when she got home.*
terminable (adj) - likely to end; can be ended	*The agreement was <u>terminable</u> should either person decide to back out.*
terminate (v) - to end; to close; to limit	*I am going to <u>terminate</u> my e-mail account and just write letters.*

Reaching the End

Choose the one word that does <u>not</u> mean the same as the first word.

1. **confine**	limit	expand	restrict
2. **definitive**	unreliable	conclusive	complete
3. **determine**	establish	decide	hesitate
4. **finale**	conclusion	culmination	commencement
5. **indeterminable**	decisive	uncertain	indefinite
6. **infinite**	measureless	limited	boundless
7. **insatiable**	quenchable	ravenous	greedy
8. **saturate**	drench	drain	soak
9. **terminate**	finish	conclude	begin

Choose the one vocabulary word that best completes the sentence.

10. The chairperson said, "The meeting will _____ after everyone has a chance to speak."
(terminable, terminate)

11. First the chairperson had to _____ how long each person could speak.
(saturate, determine)

12. Then the chairperson asked all speakers to _____ their comments to the subject of discussion. *(confine, determine)*

13. The first speaker was so unorganized that her opinion about the problem was _____.
(insatiable, indeterminable)

14. One speaker thought we had an _____ amount of money to spend on the problem.
(insatiable, infinite)

15. After all the speeches, the chairperson gave her _____ decision. *(definitive, terminable)*

Father, Mother, Birth

Root Words	Meaning	Words You Already Know
gen	birth, origin	gene
mater, matri	mother	maternity
pater, patr	father	patriot

New Words

Definitions	Sentences
expatriate (n) - a person who is forced to leave his or her native country; (v) to exile	The expatriate was forced to live in another country to avoid being tried for his crimes.
genealogy (n) - an account of ancestors and descendants	I made a family tree to show my genealogy for five generations.
genesis (n) - the beginning, origin, or way in which something was created	The genesis of her story was her recent trip to China.
genetics (n) - the branch of biology dealing with heredity	By studying genetics scientists are able to develop many cures for diseases.
maternity (adj) - concerning prospective mothers; for pregnant women	The pregnant woman shopped for maternity clothes and baby furniture.
matriarch (n) - the mother who rules the family or tribe	Rose was the matriarch of the family, and all important decisions had to be passed by her.
matrimony (n) - the act of marrying; the state of being married	Matrimony has different rituals depending on the country and religion.
matronly (adj) - like a married woman; dignified, stately	Though she was quite young, her behavior was always matronly.
paternal (adj) - fatherly; of or like a father; on the father's side of the family	His paternal grandfather was always his favorite relative.
patrician (n) - a noble, high-ranking person	Because of his wealth, the patrician had the best seats in the stadium.

Father, Mother, Birth

Fill in each line with a root word, a vocabulary word and a definition.

Root word	Vocabulary Word	Definition
1. gen		the beginning
2.	matriarch	
3. patr		to exile
4. pater		fatherly
5.	genetics	
6. mater		related to pregnancy
7.	matronly	
8. patri		high-ranking person
9. matri		marriage
10. gen		ancestry

Decide if each statement is true or false.

11. **T F** An expatriate is someone who is banished from the "fatherland."

12. **T F** A genesis is the same as a terminus.

13. **T F** If a matriarch is a mother who leads her family, a patriarch is a father who leads his family.

14. **T F** A patrician is the same as a plebeian.

15. **T F** A matronly woman is always a spinster.

16. **T F** If you trace your matrilineal ancestry, you look up your father's ancestors.

All Things Great and Small

Root Words	Meaning	Words You Already Know	
magn, magni	*great*	**magn**ify	
maxi	*large, great*	**maxi**mum	
micro	*small*	**micro**scope	
min	*small*	**min**iature	

New Words

Definitions	Sentences
diminutive (adj) - smaller than usual; tiny	*The <u>diminutive</u> kindergartner was afraid to get on the bus with the larger students.*
magnanimous (adj) - generous; not selfish; forgiving	*The <u>magnanimous</u> neighbor forgave the boys for breaking her window with their ball.*
magnate (n) - a person of great importance and with great influence	*Bill Gates, owner of Microsoft, is a <u>magnate</u> in the computer industry.*
magnificence (n) - richness; splendid appearance; beauty	*The tourists stood in awe at the <u>magnificence</u> of the cathedral.*
maximal (adj) - the greatest possible amount or size	*The <u>maximal</u> amount this bucket can hold is two liters.*
maximize (v) - to increase to the greatest possible amount	*To <u>maximize</u> his chances for a home run, he hit the ball into the left field.*
microbe (n) - a very small living thing, especially bacteria; a germ	*A small <u>microbe</u> that was found in the drinking water was responsible for the illness.*
microphone (n) - a device that changes sound waves to electrical impulses so they can be recorded or amplified	*You'll need to turn the volume down if you don't want to get a screeching noise through the <u>microphone</u>.*
mince (v) - to cut into small pieces	*<u>Mince</u> the vegetable before you put them in the water to boil.*
minuscule (adj) - very small; tiny	*The sliver was so <u>minuscule</u> that it was nearly impossible to take it out of her finger.*

All Things Great and Small

Match each word with its meaning.

1. ____ diminutive
2. ____ magnanimous
3. ____ magnificence
4. ____ maximal
5. ____ maximize
6. ____ microbe
7. ____ microphone
8. ____ magnate
9. ____ mince
10. ____ minuscule

a. V.I.P.
b. germ
c. dice
d. undersized
e. sound amplification device
f. generous
g. very small
h. splendor
i. increase
j. utmost

Answer each question. If you need more room, use the back of this paper.

11. What's the difference between a microscope and a microphone? _____

_____

12. What would you like to maximize and why? _____

_____

13. Name one person who you think is magnanimous. _____

14. Name one person who you think is a magnate. _____

15. Name something that is minuscule. _____

All About Work

Root Words	Meaning	Words You Already Know
labor	*work*	labor
oper	*work*	**oper**ate
techni	*skill*	**techni**que
trib	*pay, bestow*	con**trib**ute

New Words

Definitions	Sentences
collaborate (v) - to work with other people, especially on literary or scientific work; to cooperate with the enemy	*The scientists decided to <u>collaborate</u> and submit their findings together.*
cooperate (v) - to work together to accomplish something	*If you <u>cooperate</u> with your partner, you will be able to finish the task quickly.*
distribute (v) - to divide or give out in two or more portions; to spread out	*The teacher asked her aide to <u>distribute</u> one science kit to every two students.*
laborious (adj) - hard working; requiring a lot of labor; not easy	*She had the <u>laborious</u> task of picking up all the cards and putting them in alphabetical order.*
operable (adj) - capable of being put into use; in working condition	*Once he put a new motor in the machine, it was completely <u>operable</u> again.*
pyrotechnics (n) - the art of making or displaying fireworks	*The Chinese celebrate the new year with <u>pyrotechnics</u>.*
retribution (n) - punishment for evil doing or reward for good works	*His <u>retribution</u> for the crime was to do 100 hours of community service.*
technician (n) - one with great skill in a particular area	*Her skill in playing the violin was a combination of being a skilled <u>technician</u> and gifted artist.*
technology (n) - the science of practical or industrial arts or applied science	*<u>Technology</u> has developed many conveniences that make our lives easier.*
tribute (n) - money paid to another country or leader for protection; a gift or statement that shows respect or gratitude	*Her speech paid <u>tribute</u> to all the teachers who had helped her earn the award.*

All About Work

Choose the word that means the same or nearly the same as the first word.

1. **collaborate**   conspire   cooperate   collective
2. **distribute**   accumulate   collect   dispense
3. **laborious**   undemanding   effortless   strenuous
4. **operable**   open-minded   functional   impractical
5. **retribution**   reparation   retrenchment   reduction
6. **tribute**   dishonor   insult   commendation
7. **technician**   novice   specialist   apprentice

Use your vocabulary words to complete these sentences.

8. Computers are an innovation of _____, but you often need a _____ to keep them running.

9. Since the computer was not _____, we had the _____ task of doing the accounting the old-fashioned way.

10. Several people in the office _____ to get the task done.

11. Because the computer was inoperable, Mr. Gomez was unable to prepare and _____ the employees' paychecks on Friday.

12. When the computer was finally repaired, Mr. Gomez gave a speech, paying _____ to the repair person's skill.

13. The _____ for the person who crashed the computer was that he had to buy doughnuts for everyone on pay day.

Just Asking

Root Words	Meaning	Words You Already Know
quer, ques	*ask*	**ques**tion
quir, quis	*ask*	in**quir**e
rog	*ask, seek*	inter**rog**ate

New Words

Definitions	Sentences
acquisition (n) - the act of getting, earning, or acquiring something	His <u>acquisition</u> of old baseball cards became a profitable hobby.
arrogant (adj) - conceited, giving oneself undeserved importance	His <u>arrogant</u> manner made everyone dislike him.
derogate (v) - to lessen, especially in authority	Her ability to appear in control was <u>derogated</u> by her timid nature and soft voice.
derogatory (adj) - belittling; discrediting; humiliating	Her <u>derogatory</u> comments made Lydia feel hurt and angry.
inquest (n) - a legal investigation, especially involving a jury; a coroner's investigation	The judge ordered an <u>inquest</u> to find out why the case had been mismanaged.
inquisition (n) - an examination or investigation; an interrogation	The <u>inquisition</u> sought to find which citizens were loyal and which were not.
inquisitive (adj) - asking a lot of questions; extremely curious	The <u>inquisitive</u> child asked her parents endless questions about everything.
prerogative (n) - a right or privilege, especially acquired through rank or class	It's the queen's <u>prerogative</u> to use all the royal residences and vehicles anytime she wants.
quest (n) - a search to find or obtain something; a crusade	Their <u>quest</u> for the sunken treasure ended in disappointment.
questionable (adj) - of doubtful honesty or morality; disputable	His motives for offering help were <u>questionable</u> since he never did anything for others.

Just Asking

Replace the underlined word or words with a vocabulary word.

1. Mom conducted an <u>investigation</u> until she found out who ate all the cookies. _____

2. Her <u>haughty</u> attitude made people dislike her. _____

3. I didn't mean to <u>discredit</u> his findings by asking him so many questions. _____

4. His recent <u>purchase</u> of a new racing bike made him the envy of all his friends. _____

5. I find it very tiring to babysit for my <u>curious</u> young cousin. _____

6. The explorer's <u>exploration</u> to find a new cave was successful. _____

7. The movie review was very <u>unfavorable</u>. _____

8. Her explanation of how the car got dented was <u>disputable</u>. _____

9. The grand jury's <u>probe</u> turned up no evidence of wrongdoing. _____

10. It's my <u>right</u> to tell my sister what to do when my mom is gone. _____

Answer each question.

11. Describe a recent acquisition of yours. _____

12. An example of a derogatory comment would be when someone says _____

_____

13. Name someone who is inquisitive. _____

14. What is a prerogative that your parents have that you do not? _____

_____

15. What quest would you like to pursue? _____

_____

Life and Death

Root Words	Meaning		Words You Already Know	
mori, mort	*death*		**mort**al	
nat	*birth*		**nat**ion	
vit, viv	*life*		sur**viv**e	

New Words

Definitions	Sentences
innate (adj) - natural; inborn; not acquired	*Her ability to sing was <u>innate</u>, and she needed no training.*
international (adj) - between two or more nations	*His <u>international</u> travels took him to several countries in Europe and Africa.*
morbid (adj) - unhealthy; diseased; showing an unhealthy tendency to think about gruesome or gloomy things	*He had a <u>morbid</u> fascination with movies dealing with violence and death.*
mortify (v) - to humiliate or shame	*She was <u>mortified</u> when her mother showed her friends her baby pictures.*
naive (adj) - simple; unaffected; unsophisticated	*James was so <u>naive</u> that he believed anything his older brother told him.*
nationality (n) - membership of a particular nation either by birth or naturalization	*The traveler's <u>nationality</u> was French, but he had been living in Germany for five years.*
remorse (n) - extreme guilt for one's actions	*I feel <u>remorse</u> for saying things that hurt her feelings.*
vitalize (v) - to give life and energy to	*Her guest appearance <u>vitalized</u> the otherwise boring sitcom.*
vivacious (adj) - lively; active; spirited	*The <u>vivacious</u> youngster was the life of the party.*
vivid (adj) - bright, intense, (usually color or light); full of life.	*I have <u>vivid</u> memories of all the wonderful things we saw on the hike.*

Life and Death

Complete each sentence.

1. <u>International</u> involves more than one _____.

2. If you feel <u>remorse</u>, you feel _____.

3. If something is <u>vivid</u>, it is not _____.

4. A <u>naive</u> person would not be _____.

5. An <u>innate</u> talent is one you were _____ with.

6. If someone is <u>vivacious</u>, they are _____.

7. Your <u>nationality</u> is usually the country where you were _____.

8. If you <u>vitalize</u> something, you give it _____.

9. A <u>morbid</u> tendency is something that is generally not _____.

10. If you <u>mortify</u> someone, you _____ them.

Use your vocabulary words to complete these analogies.

11. interstate : states :: _____ : countries

12. _____ : lively :: lethargic : lifeless

13. learned : acquired :: inborn : _____

14. sophisticated : _____ :: guilty : innocent

15. ecstasy : joy :: _____ : guilt

Earth and Sea

Root Words	Meaning	Words You Already Know
aqua, aqui	*water*	**aqua**rium
geo	*land, earth*	**geo**graphy
hydr	*water*	**hydr**ant
mar, mer	*sea*	**mar**ine
terr	*land, earth*	**terr**ace

New Words

Definitions	Sentences
aquatic (adj) - living or growing in water	The <u>aquatic</u> plants made it hard to swim in the pond.
aqueduct (n) - a channel for carrying water	The <u>aqueduct</u> carried water from the wet northern region to the drier southern region.
dehydrate (v) - to become dry; to lose water	After running for a half an hour I was really <u>dehydrated</u>.
geographer (n) - a person who studies the natural features of the earth	The <u>geographer</u> mapped the area and noted all the landmarks.
geology (n) - the science that deals with rocks and the physical history of the earth	The regions's <u>geology</u> included large slabs of volcanic rock.
hydroelectric (adj) - related to electricity made from the energy of falling water	The <u>hydroelectric</u> plant included a fish ladder so fish could still return to their spawning grounds.
hydrophobia (n) - fear of water	His <u>hydrophobia</u> prevented him from ever learning how to swim.
marina (n) - a small harbor for docking small boats	The <u>marina</u> was dotted with the masts of hundreds of sail boats.
maritime (adj) - on or near the sea	The region's <u>maritime</u> industries included fishing and harvesting seaweed.
terrestrial (adj) - existing on earth; related to the world	She was a geologist who had <u>terrestrial</u> interests, while he was an astronomer who was interested in celestial objects.

Earth and Sea

Answer the following questions "yes" or "no."

1. **Yes No**   If you visit a marina, you can see boats.

2. **Yes No**   If you study geology, you study electricity.

3. **Yes No**   An aqueduct is the same as a subway.

4. **Yes No**   Hydrophobia is fear of heights.

5. **Yes No**   Hydroelectric plants are usually located on rivers.

6. **Yes No**   Terrestrial refers to things in outer space.

7. **Yes No**   When you are dehydrated, you are in need of water.

8. **Yes No**   Whales are aquatic mammals.

9. **Yes No**   A geographer is an expert on marine mammals.

10. **Yes No**   If you're visiting a maritime region, you're likely to see the ocean.

Group the following words according to whether they refer to land or water. Add two more words to each group.

aquatic	maritime	geology	dehydrate	terrestrial
terrain	geothermal	subterranean	hydraulic	marina

WATER OR SEA   LAND OR EARTH

_____   _____

_____   _____

_____   _____

_____   _____

_____   _____

_____   _____

Some Body Words

Root Words	Meaning	Words You Already Know
bio	*life*	**bio**logy
carn	*body, flesh*	**carn**ival
corp	*body*	**corp**se

New Words

Definitions	Sentences
biodegradable (adj) - able to be decomposed by biological forces, especially bacteria	*We put all the biodegradable garbage in the compost pile so it would decompose into soil.*
biography (n) - an account of a person's life that is told or written by another person	*The biography told about the athlete's early life as well as her career as a professional tennis player.*
bionic (adj) - related to things that are modeled after living organisms; having abilities improved by mechanical devices	*My grandmother jokes that with her joint replacement she is the bionic woman.*
biosphere (n) - the part of the earth where life can exist	*Without the biosphere surrounding our planet, Earth would be as lifeless as Mercury.*
carnage (n) - great destruction of life, especially in battle; slaughter	*The war zone was the site of unbelievable carnage.*
carnivorous (adj) - meat-eating	*Wolves are carnivorous, eating smaller animals but not plants.*
corporation (n) - a group of people who are joined into one legal body	*The corporation had monthly meetings of its board of directors and officers.*
corpulent (adj) - characterized by excessive body weight or stoutness	*The corpulent young boy enrolled in a weight-loss program.*
corpuscle (n) - any red or white cell that floats in the blood	*Red corpuscles carry oxygen throughout the body and white corpuscles kill harmful organisms that enter the body.*
symbiosis (n) - the shared existence of two organisms where they both benefit from living close together	*Bees and flowers exist in a state of symbiosis.*

Some Body Words

Choose the two words that best explain or define the first bold word.

1. **biodegradable**   a. bacteria   b. everlasting   c. indestructible   d. decompose

2. **biography**   a. life   b. poetry   c. fiction   d. story

3. **bionic**   a. arm   b. life-like   c. measure   d. devices

4. **biosphere**   a. atmosphere   b. death   c. life-giving   d. universe

5. **carnage**   a. killing   b. deer   c. mass   d. survival

6. **carnivorous**   a. vegetarian   b. eat   c. meat   d. tyrannosaurus

7. **corporation**   a. association   b. private   c. money   d. legal

8. **corpulent**   a. overweight   b. slender   c. stout   d. average

9. **corpuscle**   a. head   b. center   c. blood   d. cells

10. **symbiosis**   a. competing   b. together   c. living   d. parasite

Use your vocabulary words to complete these sentences.

11. The three partners formed a _____ for their business.

12. The _____ of the two sisters who lived together for fifty years and shared everything was highlighted in the magazine article.

13. We save all our _____ garbage and either compost it or recycle it.

14. Lions and tigers are _____ animals, preferring to eat meat rather than plants.

15. The scientist used a _____ arm to handle the explosive material.

Body Parts

Root Words	Meaning	Words You Already Know
cap, capit	*head*	**cap**tain
cor, cour, cord, card	*heart*	**cor**e
man	*hand*	**man**icure
ped, pod	*foot*	**ped**al, **pod**ium

New Words

Definitions	Sentences
accord (n) - agreement, harmony	*The committee quickly reached an <u>accord</u> in deciding how it should raise money.*
capitulate (v) - to surrender unconditionally	*The lieutenant waved the white flag and his troops <u>capitulated</u>.*
cardiac (adj) - related to the heart	*Another name for a heart attack is a <u>cardiac</u> arrest.*
cordial (adj) - gracious; friendly; courteous	*Her <u>cordial</u> manner made all her guests feel welcome and at ease.*
decapitate (v) - to cut the head off	*Though popular at other times in history, governments rarely <u>decapitate</u> criminals now.*
expedite (v) - to hasten, accelerate, or make something happen quicker or easier	*If you could <u>expedite</u> my order, I could get what I need and leave quickly.*
impediment (n) - something that hinders or stops the progress	*If wearing those shoes is an <u>impediment</u> to running the race, put on other shoes.*
maneuver (v) - to plan to move (especially troops); to skillfully move	*She was able to carefully <u>maneuver</u> the car into the small parking space.*
manipulate (v) - to operate with the hands; to skillfully handle	*The young child knew how to <u>manipulate</u> her parents to get what she wanted.*
pedestrian (adj) - commonplace; walking, going on foot; (n) - someone who walks	*The <u>pedestrian</u> was careful crossing the street, waiting until all cars had passed.*

Body Parts

Use the vocabulary words to fill in the missing words in these sentences.

1. The artist _____ the clay until it formed the shape of a turtle.

2. It was hard for the two men to _____ the heavy pipe into the opening.

3. After the election results were in, the loser gave a speech and _____ to his opponent.

4. Mira's mom tried to _____ her departure for school each morning by laying out all her clothes.

5. If you _____ dying blooms on your plants, it will make them produce more blossoms.

6. The _____ walked, while her friend skateboarded along beside her.

7. Her letter was _____, thanking us graciously for our help.

8. Her fear of public speaking was an _____ to running for president.

9. They reached an _____ after hours of negotiations.

10. His _____ disease forced him to change his diet and lifestyle.

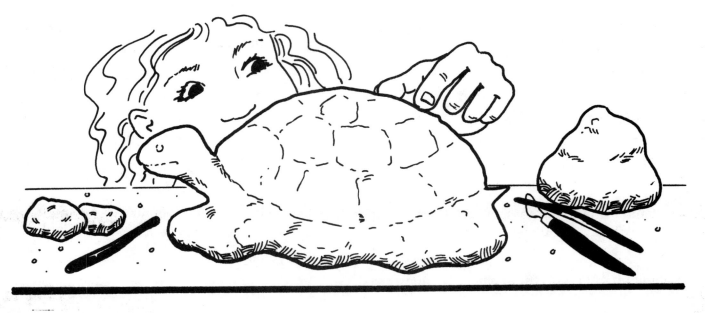

For each boldface word, choose <u>one synonym</u> and <u>one antonym</u>. Put a circle around the synonym and underline the antonym.

11. **accord**	a. musical	b. agreement	c. conflict	d. variety
12. **capitulate**	a. capitol	b. triumph	c. relentless	d. surrender
13. **cordial**	a. friendly	b. drink	c. plentiful	d. disagreeable
14. **expedite**	a. trip	b. hinder	c. speed up	d. explorer
15. **impediment**	a. force	b. assistance	c. flawless	d. obstruction

Moving

Root Words	Meaning	Words You Already Know
curr, curs	*run, course*	**curr**ent, **curs**ive
grad, gress	*move forward, step*	pro**gress**, **grad**e
mob, mov, mot	*move*	**mob**ile, **mot**ion, **mov**ement

New Words

Definitions	Sentences
concurrent (adj) - occurring at the same time; in agreement	*The meeting of the Cub Scouts and baseball practice were <u>concurrent.</u>*
currency (n) - money in circulation	*The new <u>currency</u> has bigger pictures and a metallic strip.*
cursory (adj) - careless; without close examination or attention	*He made a <u>cursory</u> attempt to correct his grammar mistakes before handing in the paper.*
digress (v) - in talking or writing, to temporarily stray from the main topic; to ramble	*Mr. Perez always <u>digresses</u> and tells us about his own experiences rather than talking about the science lesson.*
gradation (n) - the process of arranging in steps or stages; a sequence; shading	*The color of her dress was a <u>gradation</u> from light blue to navy blue.*
immobile (adj) - not moveable	*The <u>immobile</u>, abandoned car sat along the side of the road.*
mobilize (v) - to put into motion or use	*She was able to <u>mobilize</u> her plan with the help of her four friends.*
motivation (n) - the inner drive to do something or act a certain way	*While she has ability, she lacks the <u>motivation</u> to be the best.*
promotion (n) - an advancement to a higher position or rank; a forward movement	*His <u>promotion</u> to vice president came with a pay increase.*
regress (v) - to go back; to return to a previous position	*His condition <u>regressed</u> until he had to be admitted to the hospital.*

Moving

Match each vocabulary word with the correct meaning on the right.

1. ____ concurrent

2. ____ currency

3. ____ cursory

4. ____ digress

5. ____ gradation

6. ____ immobile

7. ____ mobilize

8. ____ motivation

9. ____ promotion

10. ____ regress

a. careless, hasty

b. incentive to do something

c. depart from the subject

d. put into motion, activate

e. advancement in position or rank

f. at the same time

g. move backward or lose ground

h. a gradual change through a series of stages

i. stationary, not moveable

j. money

For each sentence, find a vocabulary word to replace the underlined word or words.

11. The two bands are playing <u>at the same time</u> on two different stages. _____

12. In one play the football team's position <u>moved back</u> 15 yards. _____

13. Some mornings I lack the <u>inner drive</u> to do my piano practice before I get ready for school.

_____

14. It is not uncommon for my math teacher to <u>go off on a tangent</u> and end up talking about something entirely different. _____

15. My sister does such a <u>haphazard</u> job washing the dishes that there is often food left on them.

_____

Look and See

Root Words	Meaning	Words You Already Know
scop	*see, look*	tele**scop**e
spec, spic	*see, look*	**spec**tator
vis, vid	*see, look*	**vis**ion, **vid**eo

New Words

Definitions	Sentences
conspicuous (adj) - easily seen; noticeable	*Jered was <u>conspicuous</u> in his chicken costume.*
envision (v) - to picture in one's mind; to imagine	*I cannot <u>envision</u> what this city will be like in fifty years.*
kaleidoscope (n) - an instrument for viewing objects arranged in changing but symmetrical patterns	*The children played happily for hours with the <u>kaleidoscope</u>, watching the changing patterns.*
perspective (n) - a way of drawing objects; an evaluation of a problem by considering all the parts of the problem; an outlook or frame of mind	*The <u>perspective</u> in the painting was not completely correct, so the buildings seemed out of proportion.*
specimen (n) - part of the whole; a sample	*The scientist examined the <u>specimen</u> under the microscope.*
spectrum (n) - colored bands that are arranged by their wave lengths when a white light passes through a prism	*The <u>spectrum</u> of the rainbow changed from yellow to purple.*
speculate (v) - to think about something; viewing it from different points of view	*She <u>speculated</u> about her chances of getting the part in the play.*
visibility (n) - the ability to be seen	*The sign's <u>visibility</u> upset all the neighbors.*
vista (n) - a view or outlook	*The <u>vista</u> from the edge of the canyon was awesome.*
visual (adj) - relating to sight; used in seeing; able to be seen	*He included several <u>visual</u> aids with his report.*

Look and See

Choose the one word in each line that <u>does not</u> mean the same as the first word.

1. **conspicuous**   visible   obvious   hidden

2. **envision**   imagine   fictitious   conceive

3. **perspective**   clear   overview   viewpoint

4. **specimen**   exception   sample   example

5. **speculate**   consider   onlooker   deliberate

6. **visibility**   prominence   clearness   eyesight

7. **vista**   view   inspection   outlook

8. **visual**   imagine   relating to sight   observable

Choose the correct word to complete each sentence.

9. A _____ of color spread out across the wall from the crystal.
   (spectator, vista, spectrum)

10. Sometimes it is hard to _____ what something is like if you've never seen it before. *(envision, invisible, vista)*

11. The _____ was passed to all the children, allowing each one to see the beautiful changing patterns. *(spectrum, kaleidoscope, species)*

12. The hunter crouched behind a log, trying not to be _____.
    (visual, deceptive, conspicuous)

13. I looked at the situation from every _____ and still could not find a solution.
    (perspective, specimen, window)

14. From our porch we have a _____ of the harbor. *(illusion, vista, spectrum)*

15. I spent all night _____ about how I could get money to pay for the broken window.
    (visualizing, speaking, speculating)

        © Dandy Lion Publications - *Red Hot Root Words*

Speaking

Root Words	Meaning	Words You Already Know
dic	*say, declare*	**dic**tionary
loc, log, loqu	*speak, talk*	ventri**loqu**ist
ora	*speak*	**ora**l
test	*bear witness*	**test**ify

New Words

Definitions	Sentences
attest (v) - to certify that something is true or genuine	*I can <u>attest</u> to her innocence.*
contestable (adj) - open for debate or dispute	*While he was convinced he was right, his position was <u>contestable</u>.*
dictate (v) - to speak and have someone else write down what is said; to decree	*The doctor <u>dictated</u> his notes into a tape recorder for the secretary to transcribe later.*
dictum (n) - a statement from an authority or a judge; a saying	*The ruler's <u>dictum</u> concerning new taxes was unpopular with the peasants.*
eloquent (adj) - having fluent, powerful, vivid, graceful or persuasive speech	*His <u>eloquent</u> speech moved people to tears.*
eulogy (n) - a speech or statement of praise for a person or event	*The daughter delivered the <u>eulogy</u> at her father's funeral.*
indictment (n) - a charge or accusation	*The man's <u>indictment</u> was for four charges of forgery.*
loquacious (adj) - talkative, continually talking	*The <u>loquacious</u> boy was always getting in trouble for talking during class.*
oratory (n) - skill in public speaking	*<u>Oratory</u> was not her speciality; she did much better with the written word.*
testimonial (n) - a written statement expressing a favorable opinion	*The basketball player's <u>testimonial</u> increased sales for the product.*

Speaking

Choose the one word in each line that means the same or most nearly the same as the first word.

1. **attest**   refute   verify   quiz
2. **dictate**   order   dictator   record
3. **dictum**   instruction   diary   commandment
4. **eloquent**   articulate   ordinary   public
5. **eulogy**   criticism   praiseworthy   tribute
6. **loquacious**   lopsided   talkative   conversation
7. **testimonial**   commendation   investigation   banquet

Complete these analogies.

8. _____ : charge :: acquittal : pardon

9. _____ : debatable :: incontestable : indisputable

10. _____ : record :: speak : listen

11. _____ : favorable :: censure : ill-favored

Tell whether each statement is true or false.

12. **T   F**   A talk show host needs good oratory skills.

13. **T   F**   If something is contestable, you had better not question it.

14. **T   F**   A dictum is a request to the government for money for schools.

15. **T   F**   If you dictate an order, you make a command.

Sound Words

Root Words	Meaning	Words You Already Know
aud	*hear*	**aud**io
phon	*sound*	tele**phon**e
son	*sound*	**son**ic

New Words

Definitions	Sentences
audible (adj) - loud enough to be heard	*The puppy's whimper was barely <u>audible</u>.*
audition (n) - a hearing to test the abilities of a speaker, actor, or musician	*After the <u>audition</u> she waited in the hall to find out if she got the part.*
auditory (adj) - relating to hearing	*Listening to loud music damaged his <u>auditory</u> nerve.*
phonetics (n) - the study of speech sounds	*After studying <u>phonetics</u>, she was able to spell and read better.*
phonograph (n) - a machine to reproduce sound by using records	*The music blared from the <u>phonograph</u>.*
sonar (n) - a way of using sound to locate objects under water	*The treasure hunters used <u>sonar</u> to locate the old ship wreck on the ocean floor.*
sonnet (n) - a 14-line poem	*His <u>sonnet</u> expressed his love for his wife.*
sonorous (adj) - capable of emitting a sound, especially with a rich, full quality	*The <u>sonorous</u> tuba pumped out the melody.*
symphony (n) - a musical composition for an orchestra; harmony of sounds	*The audience sat attentively as the orchestra played the <u>symphony</u>.*
unison (n) - sounding the same note or tone at the same time; agreement; harmony	*The class sang the song in <u>unison</u>.*

Sound Words

Choose the word or phrase that completes each sentence.

1. Your <u>auditory</u> sense is your sense of *(taste, smell, hearing)*.

2. If you are reading a <u>sonnet</u>, you are reading a *(poem, novel, manual)*.

3. When the group sang in <u>unison</u>, they sang in *(tune, harmony, uniforms)*.

4. A sound that is <u>audible</u> is a sound that is *(pleasant, loud enough, too quiet)* to be heard.

5. If you are a <u>phonetic</u> expert, you know all about
   (speech sounds, animal noises, computer language).

6. <u>Sonar</u> is used for locating objects *(on mountain tops, under water, in a cave)*.

7. <u>Phonographs</u> are machines used for *(taking pictures, making graphs, playing records)*.

8. If you <u>audition</u> for a part in a play, you *(try out, are perfect, perform a dance)* for the part.

9. If you are listening to a <u>symphony</u>, you are probably listening to a group
   (sing, read poetry, play instruments).

10. If someone tells you your voice is <u>sonorous</u>, your voice is
    (whiny and irritating, rich and resonant, soft and low).

Match each word on the left with a synonym on the right.

11. ____ audible   a. resounding

12. ____ unison   b. concert

13. ____ audition   c. perceivable

14. ____ symphony   d. agreement

15. ____ sonorous   e. tryout

The Shape of Things

Root Words	Meaning	Words You already Know
cycl	*circle*	bi**cycl**e
orb	*circle*	**orb**it
sphere	*sphere*	**sphere**
rect	*straight*	**rect**angle

New Words

Definitions	Sentences
atmosphere (n) - all the air surrounding the earth	*Without the <u>atmosphere</u>, there would be no living things on Earth.*
cyclical (adj) - pertaining to or moving in a cycle	*The four seasons happen in a predictable, <u>cyclical</u> pattern.*
cyclone (n) - a violent, circular storm	*The <u>cyclone</u> did major damage to homes and businesses in the area.*
directive (n) - an instruction or order given by someone in authority	*The principal gave the <u>directive</u> for everyone to return to their classes after the fire drill.*
exorbitant (adj) - excessive; going beyond what is normal or usual	*The price for this jacket is <u>exorbitant</u>!*
hemisphere (n) - half a globe or sphere	*Europe is in the northern <u>hemisphere</u>; Australia is in the southern <u>hemisphere</u>.*
orb (n) - a sphere or globe	*The glass-covered <u>orb</u> reflected light throughout the room.*
rectify (v) - to make right; to correct something that is wrong	*She tried to <u>rectify</u> the situation by writing an apology to her friend.*
rectitude (n) - uprightness of character or conduct; honesty	*To be an Eagle Scout you must show that you have <u>rectitude</u>.*
spherical (adj) - shaped like a sphere	*The <u>spherical</u> rock turned out to be a dinosaur egg.*

The Shape of Things

Use your vocabulary words to correctly complete these sentences.

1. A ball or sphere is an _____.

2. But if you only have half a globe or sphere, you have a _____.

3. All the air surrounding the earth is the _____.

4. Anything that is shaped like a sphere is _____.

5. Someone who is decent and trustworthy has _____.

6. If you give an order, you give a _____.

7. Beware of violent storms like hurricanes, tornadoes, and _____.

8. If your purchase is overpriced, the cost is _____.

9. When you make something right, you _____ it.

10. If something happens in a recurring series, it is _____.

Choose the word or phrase that best describes or defines the first word.

11. **rectify**
    rectangular
    correct
    recover

12. **spherical**
    globular
    circular
    bell-shaped

13. **directive**
    directory
    inquisition
    dictum

14. **exorbitant**
    reasonable
    exhaustive
    excessive

15. **rectitude**
    good character
    correct manners
    strong muscles

16. **atmosphere**
    air
    water
    land

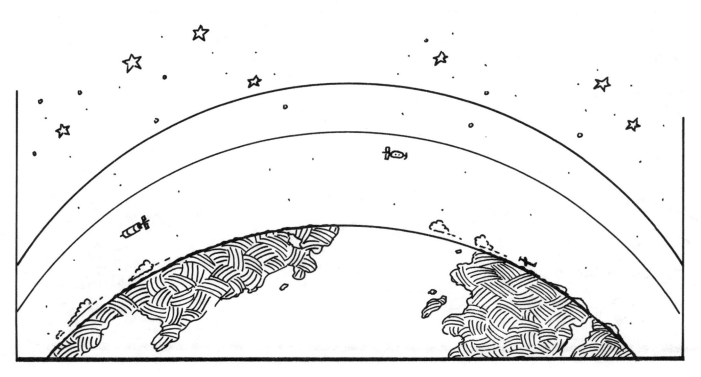

Strength and Power

Root Words	Meaning	Words You already Know
dyna, dynamo	*power*	**dyna**mite
forc, fort	*strong*	**fort**ress, **force**
pot	*power*	**pot**ential
vali, valu	*strength, worth*	**valu**e

New Words

Definitions	Sentences
dynamic (adj) - full of energy and forcefulness; related to energy or power	*The dynamic speaker soon had the whole audience on its feet clapping.*
dynamo (n) - an energetic, hard-working person	*The job needs a real dynamo who is willing to put a lot of time and energy into the project.*
dynasty (n) - a succession of rulers	*The Ming dynasty ruled China for three hundred years.*
fortify (v) - to make stronger	*They fortified the sea wall with large boulders.*
fortitude (n) - courage; endurance of pain or misfortune	*The climber's attempt to reach the summit of Mount Everest showed great fortitude.*
omnipotent (adj) - all-powerful; having great or unlimited power	*The omnipotent ruler made all decisions and had authority in all matters.*
potent (adj) - mighty; powerful; having great authority	*The hurricane was potent, destroying everything in its path.*
valid (adj) - sound or just because it is based on legal principles or sound evidence	*I gave the teacher a valid excuse for not having my homework, but she still gave me a zero.*
valor (n) - bravery; courage; fearlessness	*Because of his valor in battle, the town gave a parade in his honor.*
valorous (adj) - brave, courageous	*He received a medal of honor for his valorous conduct.*

Strength and Power

Write a vocabulary word to go with each definition.

1. _ _ _ _ _ _ _ _   strengthen and reinforce

2. _ _ _ _ _ _ _   mighty and influential

3. _ _ _ _ _ _   suitable and well-grounded

4. _ _ _ _ _ _ _   person who is a go-getter

5. _ _ _ _ _ _ _ _ _   stout-hearted and bold-spirited

6. _ _ _ _ _ _ _ _ _ _ _   all-powerful

7. _ _ _ _ _ _ _ _ _ _   courage and determination

8. _ _ _ _ _ _ _ _   energetic and forceful

9. _ _ _ _ _ _   fearlessness and bravery

10. _ _ _ _ _ _ _ _   ruling family

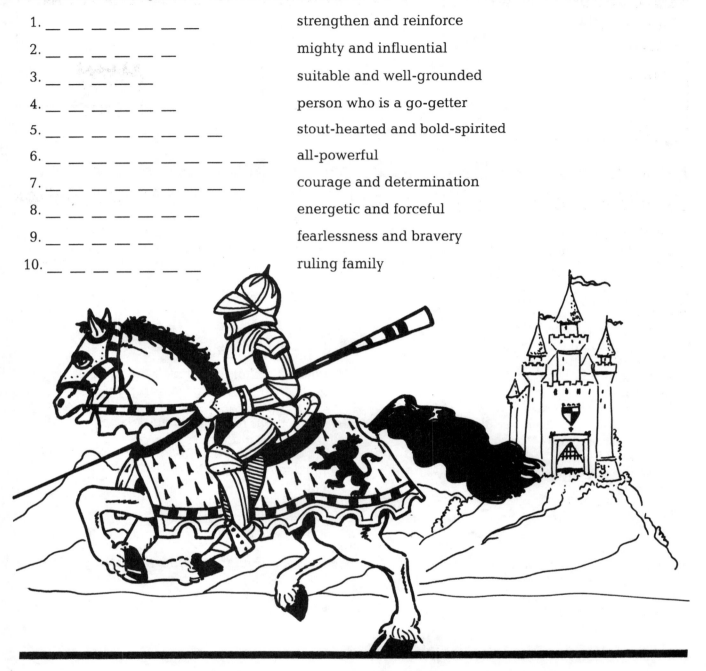

Tell whether the two words in each pair have the same or different meanings.

11. **fortitude — valor**   same   different

12. **dynamic — vigorous**   same   different

13. **fortify — weaken**   same   different

14. **potent — powerful**   same   different

15. **valid — unacceptable**   same   different

16. **fortitude — cowardice**   same   different

It's About Time

Root Words	Meaning	Words You already Know
ann, enn	*year*	**ann**iversary, cent**enn**ial
chron	*time*	**chron**icle
dai, dia	*day*	**dai**ly
jour	*day*	**jour**nal
tempo	*time*	**temp**orary

New Words

Definitions	Sentences
annual (adj) - yearly, relating to a year	*The annual meeting was held every September.*
annuity (n) - a sum of money that is payable at a certain time for a set number of years	*The annuity from his life insurance policy was paid out over ten years.*
biennial (adj) - happening every two years; lasting for two years	*The biennial reunion was slated to happen only in even-numbered years.*
chronic (adj) - continuing for a long time	*The doctor diagnosed her chronic pain as arthritis.*
chronological (adj) - arranged according to time	*The teacher gave us a list of events and asked us to put them in chronological order.*
contemporary (adj) - happening or existing at the same time; up-to-date	*The two contemporary artists were living at the same time but not in the same countries.*
diary (n) - a daily record	*I write the day's events and my feelings in my diary.*
extemporaneous (adj) - done without previous preparation	*His extemporaneous speech was inspiring considering he had no warning he would be speaking.*
journalism (n) - the work of gathering news and writing for a newspaper or periodical; journalistic writing	*His career in journalism allowed him to work for news agencies around the world.*
synchronize (v) - to make to agree in time or to happen at the same time	*Let's synchronize our watches so we can all meet at the correct time.*

© Dandy Lion Publications - *Red Hot Root Words*

105

It's About Time

Choose the vocabulary word that means the same as the underlined words or phrases.

1. As each new dancer joined the group, she made her steps <u>agree in time and tempo</u> with the other dancers' steps. _____

2. I keep a <u>daily record</u> of my thoughts and feelings. _____

3. The teacher asked the class to arrange the events <u>according to when they happened</u>. _____

4. The company issued a <u>yearly</u> report for its stockholders. _____

5. His misbehavior was a <u>continuous</u> problem. _____

6. She won the speech contest for <u>unrehearsed</u> speaking. _____

7. The family reunion was an event that happened <u>every two years</u>. _____

8. They decorated their new home in a very <u>modern</u> style. _____

9. He loved his work in <u>reporting the news</u>. _____

10. In his will, my uncle left me <u>a sum of money that is paid every year</u>. _____

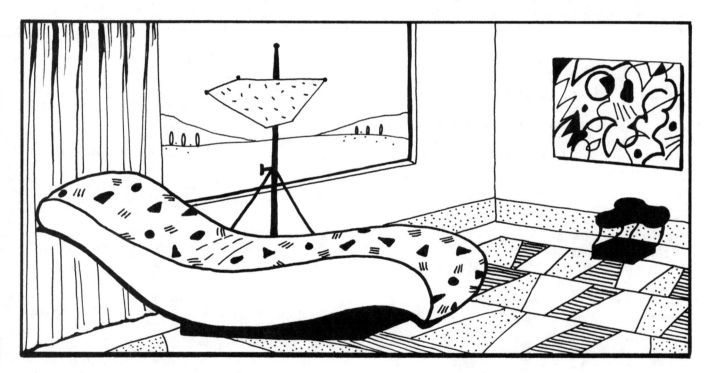

Match each word on the left with the thing it would describe or be associated with on the right.

11. ____ annual   a. historic events

12. ____ chronic   b. speaking

13. ____ chronological   c. physical exam

14. ____ journalism   d. current news events

15. ____ extemporaneous   e. pain

Twisting and Turning

Root Words	Meaning	Words You already Know
rot	*turn, wheel*	**rot**ate
tort, tors	*twist*	dis**tort**
vers, vert	*turn*	di**vert**

New Words

Definitions	Sentences
adversary (n) - a person who opposes another; an opponent	*In the story her <u>adversary</u> was her jealous, mean-spirited cousin.*
aversion (n) - a strong desire to avoid something because of feelings of dislike	*I have an <u>aversion</u> to snakes and spiders.*
contort (v) - to bend out of shape	*The gymnast was able to <u>contort</u> her body in ways that normal people could not.*
conversant (adj) - familiar (with); acquainted (with)	*The physics professor was <u>conversant</u> with the new theory, but he was not an expert.*
perversion (n) - a turning away from what is right or true; corruption	*Her <u>perversion</u> made it hard for her old friends to remain on good terms with her.*
rotation (n) - the act of turning on an axis; a regular cycle of changes; a change of places	*For each game there was a different lineup and <u>rotation</u> of batters.*
torsion (n) - the act of twisting or the state of being twisted	*By putting <u>torsion</u> on the bolt, she was able to dislodge it from the nut.*
torturous (adj) - involving torture; inflicting pain	*Dislocating your shoulder is a <u>torturous</u> experience.*
versatile (adj) - able to be easily turned or moved around; changeable; capable in many ways	*She was a <u>versatile</u> baseball player, able to play several positions.*
vertex (n) - the highest point; top	*The height of a triangle is measured from the base to the <u>vertex</u>.*

Snakes ←

Spiders →

Twisting and Turning

Match each word on the left with the word or phrase on the right with the same meaning.

1. ____ adversary
2. ____ aversion
3. ____ contort
4. ____ conversant
5. ____ perversion
6. ____ rotation
7. ____ torturous
8. ____ torsion
9. ____ vertex
10. ____ versatile

a. bend out of shape
b. abnormal behavior
c. highest point
d. movement around
e. opponent, enemy
f. having many abilities
g. the act of twisting
h. painful, unpleasant
i. opposition because of dislike
j. acquainted with

Use vocabulary words to complete these sentences.

11. If you were _____ with classical music, you would recognize the music of Bach, Beethoven and Brahms.

12. My best friend is my _____ when we are competing for the best grades.

13. Jill's _____ to snakes prevents her from enjoying hikes in the woods.

14. A Swiss army knife is a _____ implement. You can use it for many different things.

15. Having to learn the multiplication facts is a _____ experience for some students, but for others, it is not so tormenting.

Thinking and Remembering

Root Words	Meaning	Words You Already Know
intellect, intellig	*power to know*	intelligent
mem	*remember*	memory
sens	*think, perceive, feel*	sense

New Words

Definitions	Sentences
commemorate (v) - to remember or honor with a ceremony	We *commemorate* the holiday with parades and fireworks.
immemorial (adj) - very old; ancient; extending back in time beyond record or memory	When the construction crew dug the hole they found a collection of *immemorial* artifacts.
intellectual (adj) - appealing to the intellect	She prefers *intellectual* activities like reading and doing crossword puzzles rather than sports.
intellectualize (v) - to reason or think rationally, ignoring all emotions	His ability to *intellectualize* was useful in making business decisions but fell short in situations concerning his family and their feelings.
intelligible (adj) - capable of being understood	Her report was *intelligible* and neatly prepared.
memento (n) - something that is a reminder of a person or event; a souvenir	Mother let me get a statue as a *memento* of our trip to Graceland.
memoir (n) - a short biography; a scientific record	The aviator's *memoir* included fond stories of some of his memorable flights.
sensation (n) - something learned or experienced through one of the senses	After sitting with my hand in one position for a long time I lost all *sensation* in my fingers.
sensible (adj) - having or using good sense or good judgement	She was such a *sensible* child that her parents seldom had to worry about what she was doing.
sensitive (adj) - easily affected by external influences; easily hurt or annoyed	She was so *sensitive* that she cried whenever anyone teased her even a little bit.

Thinking and Remembering

Choose the word that means most nearly the same as the first word.

1. **commemorate**	overlook	memorialize	originate
2. **immemorial**	ancient	contemporary	immediate
3. **intellectual**	physical	mental	spiritual
4. **intellectualize**	understand	imagine	analyze
5. **intelligible**	understandable	incomprehensible	overbearing
6. **memento**	collection	jewelry	souvenir
7. **memoir**	love poem	life story	true confession
8. **sensation**	feeling	senseless	intuition
9. **sensible**	unsound	opinionated	practical
10. **sensitive**	thin-skinned	tough	pleasure-seeking

Choose the best word or words to complete each sentence.

11. The movie star shared several Hollywood secrets in her _____.
    (memento, memoir, invention)

12. I saw the bee and then I felt a stinging _____ on my arm.
    (sensibility, memento, sensation)

13. Because of her superior _____ abilities, she could easily learn the material with
    very little studying. *(intellectual, intelligible, athletic)*

14. The ceremony was to _____ all the people who raised money in the
    walk-a-thon. *(intellectualize, commemorate, pay off)*

15. If you're _____, you'll follow your dad's wise advice.
    (sensitive, young, sensible)

Going, Going, Gone

Root Words	Meaning	Words You Already Know
ceed, cede	go, yield	succeed, recede
ced, cess	go, separate, withdraw	recess
migr	wander	migrate

New Words

Definitions	Sentences
access (n) - an approach; a way in which something can be approached	The <u>access</u> to the beach is marked with a sign by the pathway.
concede (v) - to surrender; to admit that something is true; to give up on a disputed issue	I <u>concede</u> that you are a better tennis player than I am.
emigrant (n) - a person who leaves one country to move to another	The war forces many people to become <u>emigrants</u>, moving to other, more peaceful, regions.
immigrant (n) - a person who comes to a new country or region	The <u>immigrant</u> came to this country only five years ago.
migratory (adj) - moving from one region to another	The <u>migratory</u> birds flew from Canada to Florida in the winter.
precede (v) - to come before; to go before	May <u>precedes</u> the summer months of June, July and August.
precedent (n) - something that serves as a model, justification or example for things that happen at a later time	The court's decision set a <u>precedent</u> for future cases about this topic.
proceed (v) - to go or move, especially after stopping	After stopping at the stop sign, you can <u>proceed</u> through the intersection.
procession (n) - a number of people or things moving forward in an orderly way	The celebration included a <u>procession</u> of the queen and her princesses.
secede (v) - to withdraw formally from a group; to break off connection with others	The Civil War was a result of the Southern states <u>seceding</u> from the Union.

Going, Going, Gone

Name _____

Use vocabulary words to complete each sentence.

1. After picking your snack, _____ to the eating area.

2. If you _____ me in line, pick up a chocolate chip cookie for me.

3. After tasting all the snacks, I have to _____ that the applesauce bars are the best.

4. The only _____ to the kitchen is through the gymnasium.

5. The orderly _____ of children moved through the snack line and into the eating area.

6. Miss Smidley's class set the _____ of cleaning up trash before going to the playground.

7. During recess a _____ group of 6th grade boys moved from one area of the playground to the other.

8. Rasha is new to our class. She and her family are _____s from Egypt.

9. The girl's volleyball team said they would _____ from the intramural league if they couldn't play more games at our school.

10. When he left our country and went to live in Mexico, he became an _____.

Complete these analogies.

11. _____ : come :: emigrant : go

12. _____ : join :: migratory : stationary

13. _____ : parade :: precedent : model

14. _____ : before :: succeed : after

15. _____ : concession :: secede : secession

Take a Stand

Root Words	Meaning	Words You Already Know	
sist	*stand*	resist	
sta, stab, stat	*stand*	**sta**ble, **stag**e, **stat**ue	

New Words

Definitions	Sentences
desist (v) - to cease or discontinue	*The policeman ordered the children to <u>desist</u> writing on the wall.*
obstacle (n) - something that stands in the way	*Her inability to speak Spanish was an <u>obstacle</u> to communicating with the native people.*
obstinate (adj) - unyielding, stubborn	*The young child was extremely <u>obstinate</u>, always screaming when she did not get her way.*
persistent (adj) - to continue steadily despite opposition or obstacles	*He was <u>persistent</u> in working toward his goal of being a skilled drummer.*
stability (n) - the quality of being firm; not likely to collapse	*The <u>stability</u> of the building was undermined by the flood.*
stamina (n) - physical strength; endurance	*You'll need a lot of <u>stamina</u> in order to be able to complete the 15-mile race.*
static (adj) - unchanging	*The score between the two football teams was <u>static</u> throughout the third quarter.*
stationary (adj) - standing still; not moving	*Despite the fact that four people were pulling, the large rock remained <u>stationary</u>.*
stature (n) - the height of any object, especially a person	*His <u>stature</u> made him stand out in a crowd.*
staunch (adj) - characterize by firmness, steadfastness or stability	*She was a <u>staunch</u> supporter of the local football team.*

Take a Stand

Choose the word or words that best complete each sentence.

1. My friend, who is known to be <u>obstinate</u>, is *(friendly, stubborn, wishy-washy)*.

2. An <u>obstacle</u> is something that could *(hinder, help, hasten)* your progress.

3. If you're a <u>staunch</u> supporter of something, your support is *(lukewarm, secretive, constant)*.

4. My friend who has less <u>stature</u> than me is *(shorter, younger, stronger)* than me.

5. If you stand in a position where you are lacking <u>stability</u>, you are likely to
   (crawl, fall, stand tall).

6. Last winter the rain was <u>persistent</u>; it was *(harmless, intermittent, relentless)*.

7. When our teacher orders us to <u>desist</u> what we are doing, she wants us to
   (stop, continue, clean up).

8. When Dad says his company's profits are <u>static</u>, he means they are
   (increasing, staying the same, decreasing).

9. When my mother rides her <u>stationary</u> bicycle, the bicycle *(accelerates, vibrates, stands still)*.

10. Professional athletes have a lot of <u>stamina</u>. They have
    (physical staying power, financial security, personal trainers).

Choose the one word out of each line that <u>does not</u> mean the same as the first word.

11. **desist**	cease	suspend	detour	refrain from
12. **obstinate**	unyielding	headstrong	stubborn	flexible
13. **stability**	stableness	reliability	weakness	steadiness
14. **static**	dynamic	changeless	stagnant	motionless
15. **staunch**	firm	fickle	steadfast	faithful

Touching and Holding

Root Words	Meaning	Words You Already Know
tact, tang	*touch, feel*	con**tact**
tag, tig	*touch*	**tag**
ten, tin, tain	*hold*	ob**tain**, **ten**tacle

New Words

Definitions	Sentences
contagious (adj) - capable of being spread from one person to another	*Her laughter was <u>contagious</u>, and soon everyone was laughing.*
contiguous (adj) - touching	*France and Spain are <u>contiguous</u> countries.*
retain (v) - to keep possession of; to continue to have; to remember	*After Father's death, Mother <u>retained</u> ownership of the family business.*
sustain (v) - to maintain or keep going; to supply with necessities	*How long can you <u>sustain</u> your current schedule without getting really burned out?*
tact (n) - the ability to say or do things without offending others	*<u>Tact</u> is an important attribute for a politician who is usually trying to please voters.*
tactile (adj) - relating to or having the sense of touch	*Young children need a lot of <u>tactile</u> experiences to learn about their world.*
tangent (adj) - touching, in contact	*The dog balanced on a board that was <u>tangent</u> to a large ball.*
tangible (adj) - something that can be touched or grasped	*The diploma was a <u>tangible</u> reward for all her hard work.*
tenacious (adj) - holding fast; persistent, stubborn	*The octopus had a <u>tenacious</u> hold on the crab.*
tenant (n) - a person who rents property from another person and lives in the property	*The <u>tenant</u> never paid his rent on time, which angered the landlord.*

Touching and Holding

Answer each question. If you need more room, use the back of this paper.

1. Name two things that are contagious. _____

2. Name two things that are not tangible. _____

3. Draw two figures that are contiguous.

Tell whether the following statements are true or false.

4. **T F** If you retain something, you give it away.

5. **T F** People with tact often hurt other people's feelings.

6. **T F** If you're tenacious, you don't give up.

7. **T F** If you're a tenant you have to pay rent.

8. **T F** Tactile refers to your sense of taste.

9. **T F** If two things are tangent, they are parallel to each other.

10. **T F** If you sustain your efforts, you give up easily.

Match the word on the left with a synonym on the right.

11. ____ contagious   a. tangent

12. ____ contiguous   b. persevering

13. ____ sustain   c. diplomacy

14. ____ tenacious   d. keep up

15. ____ tact   e. transmittable

Governmental Words

Root Words	Meaning	Words You Already Know
crac, cracy	*rule, power*	demo**cracy**
dom	*rule, power*	**dom**inate
feder, fid	*faith, trust*	**feder**al, con**fide**

New Words

Definitions	Sentences
affidavit (n) - a statement (usually written) made under oath	*He signed an <u>affidavit</u> claiming to be the real owner of the property.*
aristocracy (n) - people in the upper class; a government run by the upper class	*The citizens revolted against the <u>aristocracy</u> and formed a government that represented all citizens, regardless of wealth or social standing.*
autocrat (n) - a ruler with unlimited powers	*While the <u>autocrat</u> had ultimate power, he truly tried to treat his people well.*
confident (adj) - self-assured; having full trust	*I am <u>confident</u> that you will be able to do it.*
confidential (adj) - secretive or relating to secret matters	*What I am about to tell you is strictly <u>confidential</u>. Don't tell anyone.*
domineering (adj) - overbearing; inclined to rule with arrogance	*<u>Domineering</u> people often get their way, but everyone thinks they are bullies.*
dominion (n) - supreme authority; an empire	*The king had <u>dominion</u> over the entire country.*
federation (n) - a union; a league of individual people or states	*As a group, the <u>federation</u> decided to send aid to the war-torn country.*
fidelity (n) - faithfulness; loyalty; belief	*<u>Fidelity</u> is a key ingredient of good friendships and marriages.*
infidel (n) - an unbeliever; someone who has no faith	*The <u>infidel</u> was banished from the church.*

Governmental Words

For each sentence, find a vocabulary word to replace the underlined word or phrase.

1. The <u>dictator</u> made all the final decisions but listened to the recommendations of his advisors.

   _____

2. The queen's <u>realm</u> included her country and several smaller, adjoining territories.

   _____

3. She rewarded her subject's <u>loyalty</u> with high wages and protection from the enemy.

   _____

4. Though a member of the <u>nobility</u>, Sir James had many friends who were common people.

   _____

5. What she told me was <u>secret</u>, so I can't tell you. _____

Match each word on the right with a definition on the left.

6. ____ affidavit	a. absolute ruler
7. ____ aristocracy	b. not to be disclosed, hush-hush
8. ____ autocrat	c. united group
9. ____ confident	d. unbeliever
10. ____ confidential	e. authority, power, jurisdiction
11. ____ domineering	f. loyalty, faithfulness
12. ____ dominion	g. sure; certain; sure of oneself
13. ____ federation	h. sworn statement
14. ____ fidelity	i. nobility; government by people of a privileged class
15. ____ infidel	j. bossy, dictatorial, harsh

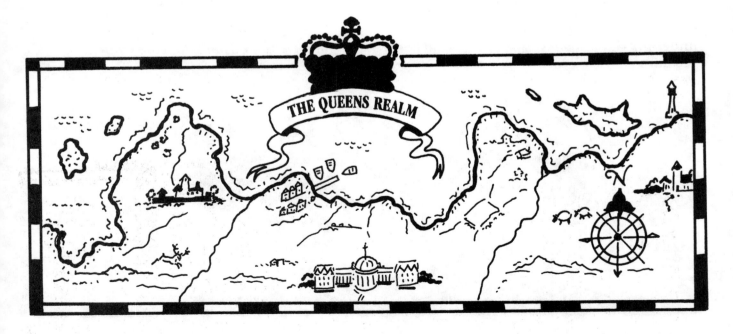

THE QUEENS REALM

People

Root Words	Meaning	Words You Already Know
dem, demo	*people*	**dem**ocracy
greg	*group, crowd*	con**greg**ation
hum	*man*	**hum**an
pop	*people*	**pop**ulation

New Words

Definitions	Sentences
aggregate (n) - formed by the collection of several things into a whole group	*His collection was an <u>aggregate</u> of baseball cards, autographs, and pictures.*
demagogue (n) - a person who gains power by arousing people's emotions and prejudices; a troublemaker	*Hitler was a <u>demagogue</u> who used his power in inhumane ways.*
demographics (n) - information about a population	*The <u>demographics</u> showed that there was a decrease in the percentage of children.*
gregarious (adj) - sociable, fond of being with other people	*His <u>gregarious</u> personality made him popular with a lot of people.*
humane (adj) - characterize by compassion and sympathy for people	*The <u>humane</u> thing to do would be to forgive her.*
humanitarian (adj) - having concern for and the willingness to help other people	*The group's <u>humanitarian</u> efforts included sending food and medical supplies to the earthquake victims.*
philanthropy (n) - affection for mankind, usually demonstrated by donations of money	*Her <u>philanthropy</u> was recognized with a monument in the town square.*
populace (n) - people who live in a particular place	*The <u>populace</u> of this region is mostly farmers.*
populous (adj) - heavy populated; inhabited by a lot of people	*New York City and Hong Kong are <u>populous</u> cities.*
segregate (v) - to isolate or separate from the main group	*<u>Segregate</u> the rotten fruit so it won't spoil the good fruit.*

People

Find the one word in each line that <u>does not</u> mean the same as the first word.

1. **aggregate**	collection	mixture	combination	rock
2. **demagogue**	rabble-rouser	temple	agitator	troublemaker
3. **humane**	warmhearted	compassionate	ruthless	sympathetic
4. **humanitarian**	merciless	big-hearted	helpful	generous
5. **gregarious**	outgoing	solitary	friendly	affable
6. **philanthropy**	charity	generosity	benevolence	wealth
7. **populace**	inhabitants	residents	peasants	citizenry
8. **segregate**	fuse	separate	isolate	seclude

Answer each question. If you need more room, use the back of this paper.

9. What's the most populous place you've ever visited? _____

10. What are three things that might be included in the demographics of your class? _____

_____

11. Name one person who you think is gregarious. _____

12. Describe one time when your actions were humane. _____

Tell whether each statement is true or false.

13. **T F** A demagogue is a peacemaker.

14. **T F** If you're gregarious, you would rather be with people than be alone.

15. **T F** A populous area is sparsely populated.

Listing of Root Words

Root Words	Meaning	Sample Words
acou	*hear, sound*	acoustic, acoustics
act	*go, do*	active, activity, activate, act, action, activist
ag	*do, act*	agenda, agitate, litigate, agile
ann, enn	*year*	See Lesson 36
anthro	*man, human being*	anthropology, anthropoid, misanthrope, philanthropy, philanthropist
apt, ept	*fit*	apt, adaptable, adept, adaptation, aptitude, inept
aqua, aqui	*water*	See Lesson 27
arch	*rule, leader, chief*	architect, anarchy, matriarch, patriarch monarch, oligarchy, archangel
aud	*hear*	See Lesson 33
auto	*same, self*	autograph, automatic, automate, automobile, autonomy, autobiography
bell	*war*	antebellum, rebellion, bellicose, belligerent
bio	*life*	See Lesson 28
calor	*heat*	calorie
cap, capit	*head*	See Lesson 29
cap	*seize*	capture, captive, captivate, capable, captious, caption
carn	*body, flesh*	See Lesson 28
caust	*burn*	holocaust, caustic, cauterize
ced, cess	*go, separate, withdraw*	See Lesson 39
ceed, cede	*go, yield*	See Lesson 39
cent	*one hundred*	cent, century, centigrade, centurion, centimeter, centipede, percent
cep, cept	*take, receive*	accept, exception, deceptive, perceptive, reception, receptive
chron	*time*	See Lesson 36
cid, cis	*cut*	scissors, decide, concise, decisive, incisor, incise, decidedly, excise, homicide, incision

Root Words	Meaning	Sample Words
clam, claim	*cry out*	exclaim, exclamation, clamor, clamorous, proclamation, acclaim, declamatory, claimant
clud, clus	*shut*	conclusion, conclusive, seclusion, recluse, exclude, exclusive, include, preclude, reclusive
cor, cour, cord, card	*heart*	See Lesson 29
corp	*body*	See Lesson 28
crac, cracy	*rule, power*	See Lesson 42
creat	*create*	create, creative, recreation, procreate, re-create, creature, creator, creation
cred	*believe*	credence, credible, incredulous, accreditation, credential, credibility, creed, discredit, incredible, credulous
curr, curs	*run, course*	See Lesson 30
cus, cuse, cause	*cause, motive*	excuse, because, causative, causation
cycl	*circle*	See Lesson 34
dai, dia	*day*	See Lesson 36
dem, demo	*people*	See Lesson 43
dic	*say, declare*	See Lesson 32
doc	*teach*	doctrine, documentation, indoctrinate, docent, docile, doctor, documentary, docudrama, document
dom	*rule, power*	See Lesson 42
dorm	*sleep*	dormitory, dormer, dormant, dormancy, dormouse
duc	*lead*	educate, conducive, deduction, induce, seduce
dyna, dynamo	*power*	See Lesson 35
fect, fic, fac	*make*	effect, fiction, proficient, benefactor, facile, infect, factory
feder, fid	*faith, trust*	See Lesson 42
fin	*end*	See Lesson 21
flam	*fire*	flame, flamboyant, flammable, inflame, flaming, flameproof, flamingo, inflammatory

Root Words	Meaning	Sample Words
flex, flect	*bend*	reflection, flexible, deflect, inflection, inflexible, flex, flexibility, genuflection, reflexive
flu	*flow*	fluid, influx, flume, fluent, fluctuate, flux, effluent
form	*shape, form*	conform, deform, conformity, format, formula, formative, formal
fort, forc	*strong*	See lesson 35
frag, fract	*break, shatter*	fragment, fracture, fraction, fragile, infraction, refraction
fum	*smoke*	fume, fuming, fumigate, fumigation, fumigator, fumid
gen	*birth, origin*	See Lesson 22
gen	*kind of*	genuine, genus, generic, general, generality, generalization, genre
geo	*land, earth*	See Lesson 27
gni, gno	*learn*	agnostic, cognizance, ignorance, incognito, cognition, cognitive, diagnosis, prognosis, gnome, incognizant, ignorance, ignorant, prognostic, recognize
grad, gress	*move forward, step*	See Lesson 30
graph, gram	*write, writing*	See Lesson 20
grat	*please, pleasing*	gratify, gratitude, gratuity, gratuitous, grateful, gratification, ingrate
grav	heavy	gravity, grave, gravitate, gravitational
greg	*group, crowd*	See Lesson 43
hab	*live*	habitat, habitable, habitation, inhabit, habitable, inhabitant
habit, hibit	*have, hold*	exhibit, habit, habitual, inhibit, inhibition prohibit
hosp, host	*guest, host*	hostess, hospital, hospice, hostage, hostel, inhospitable, hospitality
hum	*man*	See Lesson 43
hydr	*water*	See Lesson 27
hypno	*sleep*	hypnotize, hypnotic, hypnosis, hypnotherapy
ign	*fire*	ignite, ignition, igneous, ignitable

Root Words	Meaning	Sample Words
intellect, intellig	*power to know*	See Lesson 38
ject	*throw*	reject, projectile, eject, conjecture, dejected, trajectory
jour	*day*	See Lesson 36
jud, jur, jus	*law, justice*	judge, justice, jury, judicial, jurisdiction, justifiable, abjure, adjudicate, judiciously, judiciousness, jurisprudence, jurist, juror, prejudice, perjury justification, justify
junct	*join*	junction, adjunct, juncture, injunction
labor	*work*	See Lesson 24
lav	*wash*	lavatory, lava, lavation, lavish, lavishness
leg	*law*	legal, legality, legislate, legislative, legitimate, illegal, illegitimate, legal tender, legalize
lev	*light*	levity, leavening, alleviate, alleviate, levitate, lever, elevate
liber, liver	*free*	liberty, liberate, liberator, liberal
lit, liter, letter	*letter*	literature, alliteration, literary, literacy, literally, literal, letterhead, lettered, letter-perfect
loc	*place*	location, dislocate, localize, relocate, allocate, local, locale, locality, locomotion
loc, log, loqu	*speak, talk*	See Lesson 32
luc, lum	*light*	lumen, translucent, lucite, lucid, lucent, luminary, luminance, luminescence, luminous, luminosity
magn, magni	*great*	See Lesson 23
man	*hand*	See Lesson 29
mar, mer	*sea*	See Lesson 27
mater, matri	*mother*	See Lesson 22
maxi	*large, great*	See Lesson 23
mem	*remember*	See Lesson 38
mens	*measure*	measure, commensurate, dimension, immense, measurable
meter	*measure*	speedometer, thermometer, altimeter, barometer, odometer, centimeter, iambic pentameter

Root Words	Meaning	Sample Words
micro	*small*	See Lesson 23
migr	*wander*	See Lesson 39
mill	*thousand*	million, millimeter, millennium, millipede, millennial, millenarian, milligram
min	*small*	See Lesson 23
miss, mit	*send*	mission, transmit, intermittent, missile, emit, remit, submit
mob, mot, mov	*move*	See Lesson 30
monstr	*show*	demonstrate, demonstrative, demonstrator, remonstrate
mori, mort	*death*	See Lesson 26
nat	*birth*	See Lesson 26
noct	*night*	nocturnal, nocturne, noctilucent, noctiflorous, equinox
nov	*new*	novelty, novel, novice, novation, nova
nunci, nounc	*warn, declare*	announce, renounce, enunciate
oper	*work*	See Lesson 24
ora	*speak*	See Lesson 32
orb	*circle*	See Lesson 34
pac	*peace*	pacify, Pacific, pacifier, pacification
part	*part*	particle, apartment, compartment, partisan, participle, impartial, partition, participate, partial, partner
pater, patr	*father*	See Lesson 22
ped, pod	*foot*	See Lesson 29
ped	*child*	pediatrics, pedagogue, pediatrician
pel, pulse	*move or drive*	impulse, impulsive, repulse, pulse, expel, compel, propeller, pulsate, propulsion
pend	*hang, weigh*	suspend, pendulum, pending, suspenders
phil	*love*	Philadelphia, philanthropy, philosophy, bibliophile
phon	*sound*	See Lesson 33
photo	*light*	photography, photocopy, photogenic, photon, telephoto, photosynthesis
pict	*paint*	picture, picturesque, pictograph, pictorial

Root Words	Meaning	Sample Words
pli, ply, plex	*fold*	pliers, multiply, complex, pliable, plight, replicate, implicit, plexiglass, pliant, ply, replica, reply, plywood
pop	*people*	See Lesson 43
port	*bring, carry*	See Lesson 19
pos	*place*	position, pose, positive, posture, post
pot	*power*	See lesson 35
prim	*first*	primary, primal, primer, primordial, primitive, prime, prima donna, primrose, prime minister
punct	*point*	punctuate, puncture, punctual, acupuncture
pyro	*fire*	pyrotechnics, pyromania, pyre, pyretic, Pyrex
quer, ques	*ask*	See Lesson 25
quir, quis	*ask*	See Lesson 25
rect	*straight*	See Lesson 34
ridi, risi	*laugh*	ridicule, ridiculous, risible
rog	*ask, seek*	See Lesson 25
rot	*turn, wheel*	See Lesson 37
sacr, sant	*holy*	sacred, sacrilege, sanctify, sanctimonious, desecrate, sacrament, sacrifice, sacrilegious, sacrosanct, sanction, sanctuary
sat	*enough*	See Lesson 21
sci	*know*	science, conscience, omniscience, conscientious
scrib, scrip	*write, writing*	See Lesson 20
scrut	*see, look*	scrutinize, scrutiny, scrutable
sect	*cut*	section, bisect, dissect, intersect, sector, intersection, transect, trisect
sens	*think, perceive, feel*	See Lesson 38
simil, simul	*like*	similar, simultaneous, facsimile, assimilate, simile, simulation
sist	*stand*	See Lesson 40
somn, sopor	*sleep*	insomnia, comatose

Root Words	Meaning	Sample Words
son	*sound*	See Lesson 33
soph	*wise, wisdom*	philosopher, sophist, sophomore
spec, spic, scop	*see, look*	See Lesson 31
sphere	*sphere*	See Lesson 34
spond, spons	*answer, pledge*	respond, sponsor, responsive, irresponsible, correspondence, corresponding, unresponsive
sta, stab, stat	*stand*	See Lesson 40
stru, struct	*build*	See Lesson 19
sume, sumpt	*take, receive*	resume, assumption, assume, presumption, consumption, consumer, consumerism
tact, tang	*touch*	See Lesson 41
tag, tig	*touch*	See Lesson 41
techni	*skill*	See Lesson 24
temper	*temperature*	temper, temperate, temperature
tempo	*time*	See Lesson 36
ten, tin, tain	*hold*	See Lesson 41
tend, tens, tent	*stretch*	attention, contentious, detente, distend, extend, extenuating, intensity, pretense, tension
term	*end*	See Lesson 21
terr	*land, earth*	See Lesson 27
test	*bear witness*	See Lesson 32
text	*weave*	texture, textile, context
the, theo	*god*	theocracy, theological, theocentric, theologian, theology
therm	*heat*	thermos, thermometer, thermostat, thermal
tort, tors	*twist*	See Lesson 37
tract	*pull, draw*	tractor, detract, protract, retract, attraction, distraction, contract, traction, intractable, tract
trib	*pay, bestow*	See Lesson 24
tui, tut	*teach*	tutor, tutelage, tuition, tutorial

Root Words	Meaning	Sample Words
vac	*empty*	vacuum, vacancy, vacuous, evacuate, evacuee, vacant, vacate, vacation
vali, valu	*strength, worth*	See lesson 35
ven, vent	*come*	event, advent, adventure, venture, adventurous
ver	*truth*	verify, veracity, verdict, verisimilar, verification
vers, vert	*turn*	See Lesson 37
vinc, vict	*conquer*	victim, victor, invincible, victimize, provincial
vis, vid	*see, look*	See Lesson 31
vit, viv	*life*	See Lesson 26
voc, vok	*speak, voice, call*	vocal, evoke, vocation, vociferate, equivocate, provoke, vociferous, provocation, vocalize, invocation
volcan, vul	*burn*	volcano, volcanic, vulcanize
volu, volv	*turn around*	revolution, revolve, evolution, convolution, convoluted
vor	*eat*	carnivore, carnivorous, omnivore, voracious, herbivore

Able and Capable

Suffixes	Meaning	Words You Already Know
able, ible	*able, can do*	enjoy**able**
il, ile	*capable of being, like*	frag**ile**

New Words

Definitions	Sentences
civil (adj) - polite and respectful; acting with courtesy and civility	*Though his customer was angry, the sales clerk handled his complaint in a <u>civil</u> manner.*
docile (adj) - easy to manage; gentle; easy to teach or discipline	*Jorge was a calm, <u>docile</u> child, unlike his twin sister, who was unruly and rebellious.*
edible (adj) - able to be eaten	*Artichokes are <u>edible</u> thistles.*
futile (adj) - useless; ineffective; incapable of producing the desired effect	*His efforts to remove the stump were <u>futile</u>. It would not budge.*
hospitable (adj) - treating people with kindness, generosity and attention	*The inn was noted for its <u>hospitable</u> employees and excellent food.*
intangible (adj) - not able to be touched or measured; not definite or concrete	*While love is <u>intangible</u>, there are many concrete ways that you can show your love.*
laughable (adj) - causing laughter and amusement; amusing	*Mom's first attempt to roller blade was <u>laughable</u>.*
portable (adj) - able to be moved to another location	*The basketball hoop was <u>portable</u>, allowing it to be used on the playground or in the gym.*
tenable (adj) - able to be held, maintained or defended	*She gave a <u>tenable</u> argument for changing the recess schedule, but the principal rejected it.*
volatile (adj) - changeable; easy to explode	*She had a <u>volatile</u> temper, often flying off the handle for no apparent reason.*

Able and Capable

Choose the one word in each line that <u>does not</u> mean the same as the first word.

1. **civil**	courteous	religious	public	well-mannered
2. **hospitable**	cordial	amicable	friendly	sanitary
3. **intangible**	abstract	vague	concrete	untouchable
4. **portable**	absorbent	movable	transferable	transportable
5. **tenable**	defendable	viable	irrational	justifiable
6. **volatile**	unstable	peaceful	explosive	changeable

Choose the correct vocabulary word to complete the sentence.

7. She was such a _____ child that she was no trouble to babysit.
   (*volatile, docile, laughable*)

8. While the dish was _____, it wasn't something I really liked eating.
   (*edible, portable, civil*)

9. The clown's _____ behavior made all the youngsters in the audience giggle.
   (*civil, hospitable, laughable*)

10. It's _____ *for you to try to convince her. I know she will not change her mind.*
    (*futile, tenable, laughable*)

Match each word with a definition on the right.

11. ____ docile   a. kind and attentive to other people

12. ____ volatile   b. able to be touched

13. ____ tangible   c. able to be defended

14. ____ tenable   d. changeable or explosive

15. ____ hospitable   e. obedient and agreeable

It's Like

Suffixes	Meaning	Words You Already Know
al	*like, pertaining to*	us**al**, natur**al**
ine	*like, pertaining to*	mascul**ine**, genu**ine**
ous	*like, pertaining to*	myster**ious**, delic**ious**

New Words

Definitions	Sentences
autumnal (adj) - characteristic of autumn; blooming in autumn	*While it was only August, the weather was very* <u>*autumnal*</u>*: crisp, damp and cold.*
elephantine (adj) - large and clumsy; resembling an elephant	*The* <u>*elephantine*</u> *sea lion was graceful in the water but clumsy on land.*
malicious (adj) - characterized by ill will with the desire to cause harm; spiteful	<u>*Malicious*</u> *gossip hurts the person who spreads it as well as the person it is about.*
phenomenal (adj) - extraordinary; pertaining to strange, uncommon or remarkable things	*The store had* <u>*phenomenal*</u> *business the first day it opened.*
political (adj) - concerning politics and government	*His* <u>*political*</u> *career included being a governor and a senator.*
pristine (adj) - pertaining to an earlier state or condition; original	*When she opened the antique trunk, she found many old clothes in* <u>*pristine*</u> *condition.*
saccharine (adj) - sweet; sugary	*Her* <u>*saccharine*</u> *personality made people feel that she was not genuine.*
serpentine (adj) - like a snake; winding; crafty	*The* <u>*serpentine*</u> *river wound its way through the hilly countryside.*
slanderous (adj) - related to false statements made about someone	*The mayor was angry that someone in town was making statements about him that he considered* <u>*slanderous*</u>*.*
voracious (adj) - greedy; unable to be satisfied; eager to eat a lot of food	*The football players had* <u>*voracious*</u> *appetites after each practice.*

It's Like

Tell whether the two words in each line have the same or different meanings.

1. slanderous - malicious   same   different
2. elephantine - petite   same   different
3. phenomenal - extraordinary   same   different
4. voracious - ravenous   same   different
5. malicious - kindhearted   same   different
6. pristine - unspoiled   same   different
7. serpentine - meandering   same   different
8. autumnal - equinox   same   different
9. saccharine - sour   same   different
10. political - governmental   same   different

Decide whether the following statements are true or false.

11. **T F** If you have a saccharine personality, you are a dour, cheerless person.

12. **T F** A serpentine route is the shortest distance between two points.

13. **T F** If you find a treasure that is pristine, you have found something that has not changed much from its original condition.

14. **T F** A malicious statement could also be considered a spiteful statement.

15. **T F** If you have a voracious appetite, you are not very hungry.

More Like Words

Suffixes	Meaning	Words You Already Know
ic	*like, pertaining to*	artist**ic**, hero**ic**
ical	*like, pertaining to*	polit**ical**, mus**ical**
ive	*like, pertaining to*	act**ive**, explos**ive**

New Words

Definitions	Sentences
affirmative (adj) - positive; stating a position in favor of something	*Dad's answer was <u>affirmative</u>, giving his approval to our plan.*
barbaric (adj) - crude; related to people who act in a rude, uncivilized way	*The small child's behavior was <u>barbaric</u>, but she had never learned how to behave in a restaurant.*
cohesive (adj) - related to sticking together; connected, sticking	*The <u>cohesive</u> properties of this glue are better than the tape.*
critical (adj) - inclined to find fault; related to a crisis	*My neighbor is so <u>critical</u>. She complains about everyone on the block.*
evocative (adj) - pertaining to calling forth, summoning, or bringing out	*The minister's <u>evocative</u> sermon moved several people to tears.*
hysterical (adj) - very emotional and out of control	*She became <u>hysterical</u> when she noticed the spider on her arm.*
objective (adj) - pertaining to facts rather than feelings; real; without prejudice	*Try to be <u>objective</u> about this rather than letting your emotions interfere.*
prolific (adj) - to produce abundant ideas, work, fruit or offspring	*The <u>prolific</u> writer turned out two books a year in addition to several magazine articles.*
rustic (adj) - unsophisticated; unpolished; rough; related to rural living	*While the cabin was <u>rustic</u>, it did have running water and electricity.*
simplistic (adj) - uncomplicated, oversimplified	*His <u>simplistic</u> view of things meant that he didn't always see all sides of the issue.*

More Like Words

For each sentence, find a vocabulary word to replace the underlined word or phrase.

1. The small child was <u>beside herself</u> whenever she was left with a babysitter. _____

2. The voters gave an <u>approving</u> vote for the school tax. _____

3. My grandmother, who is a avid seamstress, has produced an <u>abundant</u> collection of quilts. _____

4. Her report on the stock market was <u>lacking in complexity</u>, perhaps because she did not understand the subject. _____

5. Because of his <u>uncouth</u> behavior, he will never be invited to one of Lady Pearl's dinner parties again. _____

6. The report on the company's safety procedures was a <u>faultfinding</u> account. _____

7. Please give me you <u>impartial, unbiased</u> opinion. _____

8. The painting depicted a <u>pastoral</u> scene. _____

9. Which is more <u>sticky</u>, paste or glue? _____

10. The scent of the perfume was <u>suggestive</u> of fresh cut spring flowers. _____

Answer each question. Use the back of this piece of paper.

11. Give the name of one person who is sometimes critical.

12. State three questions that you could answer in the affirmative.

13. List five things that are cohesive.

14. Give two situations that would cause you to be hysterical.

15. Describe two behaviors that would be considered barbaric.

With and Without

Suffixes	Meaning	Words You Already Know
ful	*full of*	joy**ful**, wonder**ful**
less	*without*	fear**less**
ose, **ous**	*full of, excessive*	joy**ous**, grandi**ose**

New Words

Definitions	Sentences
bellicose (adj) - very quarrelsome; full of hostility; inclined to fight	*The bull was in a <u>bellicose</u> mood and charged at the boys who teased it.*
doubtful (adj) - full of uncertainty; undecided	*It's <u>doubtful</u> that you'll be able to go, but it won't hurt to ask.*
dutiful (adj) - obedient; full of an obligation to fulfill one's duty	*She was such a <u>dutiful</u> child, always doing what her parents requested and expected.*
effortless (adj) - easy; not requiring mental or physical exertion	*Lifting the heavy rock was an <u>effortless</u> task for the muscular man.*
joyless (adj) - gloomy; without joy or gladness; full of desperation	*Hers was a <u>joyless</u> life, full of disappointments and sadness.*
merciful (adj) - full of mercy or willingness to forgive; compassionate; charitable	*My neighbor is the kindest, most <u>merciful</u> person you would ever want to meet.*
morose (adj) - gloomy; unsociable; tending to be sulky	*His <u>morose</u> personality meant that other people found it difficult to be around him.*
pitiful (adj) - deserving or calling forth pity; miserable; sorrowful	*What a <u>pitiful</u> sight it was! There sat our cat dripping wet and shaking with cold.*
vengeful (adj) - full of a need to get even or repay an injury or an offense	*It is usually better to be forgiving than to be <u>vengeful</u>.*
verbose (adj) - using more words than are necessary	*My science teacher is <u>verbose</u>. You usually fall asleep before he finishes his explanation.*

With and Without

Use vocabulary words to complete the following sentences.

1. I was graded down on my essay because it was too _____. Miss Sanchez wanted a concise explanation.

2. She skated with such ease that she made it seem _____.

3. After the death of his dog, Jake was _____ and withdrawn.

4. The newspaper article painted a _____ picture of the plight of older people in our community, arousing feelings of sympathy and prompting efforts to improve conditions.

5. My mother's approval is _____. I'm not certain she will say yes.

6. While one of the victims was _____ and willing to forgive; the other victim was _____ and wanted to get even with the assailant.

7. While most people would see her work as _____, Sister Teresa found great satisfaction and happiness in helping other people.

8. My father got an award for being a _____ employee. They said he was always respectful, reliable, and agreeable.

9. I don't like playing with Josh because he gets so aggressive and _____, especially when he thinks he might lose.

Match each word below with the words that mean the <u>opposite</u>.

10. ____ bellicose

11. ____ vengeful

12. ____ morose

13. ____ doubtful ✓

14. ____ joyless ✓

15. ____ verbose ✓

a. definite and decided

b. cheerful and good-natured

c. succinct and terse

d. peaceful and noncombatant

e. merciful and forgiving

f. pleasurable, gratifying

Resembling

Suffixes	Meaning	Words You Already Know
ish	*resembling, like*	child**ish**
ly	*resembling, like*	man**ly**
oid	*resembling, like*	spher**oid**
some	*resembling, like*	hand**some**

New Words

Definitions	Sentences
amateurish (adj) - like an amateur; crude; lacking professional finish	*The <u>amateurish</u> video was amusing even if it was imperfect.*
anthropoid (adj) - resembling a human being, especially when referring to the most highly developed apes	*Gorillas, orangutans and chimpanzees have some <u>anthropoid</u> features.*
asteroid (n) - small celestial bodies that revolve around the sun	*We were able to see the <u>asteroid</u> shower without using a telescope.*
brutish (adj) - savage and stupid; like a cruel, insensitive person	*Her <u>brutish</u> behavior made everyone fear her; but no one respected her.*
loathsome (adj) - disgusting, revolting; causing great dislike	*I think taking out the garbage is a <u>loathsome</u> task.*
prudish (adj) - excessively proper or modest	*My grandmother was a <u>prudish</u> woman, always concerned about what was proper.*
quarrelsome (adj) - inclined to argue or disagree	*My sister has a very <u>quarrelsome</u> nature, so it's hard to carry on a civil conversation with her.*
saintly (adj) - like a saint; patient and caring	*My second grade teacher was <u>saintly</u>. She was always so kind and caring.*
tabloid (n) - a smaller version of a newspaper, often with more sensational news.	*You will find the <u>tabloids</u> sold next to the check out stand at the market.*
winsome (adj) - charming, engaging	*Her <u>winsome</u> ways won the hearts of everyone she met.*

Resembling

Choose the best word or phrase that completes each sentence.

1. Someone who behaves in a <u>saintly</u> manner is (*pitiful, pious, self-righteous*).

2. When someone says, "Don't be so <u>quarrelsome</u>," they want you to be more (*belligerent, querulous, amiable*).

3. Something that is <u>anthropoid</u>, resembles (*humans, anthropologists, apes*).

4. An <u>asteroid</u> is a (*common flower, small planet, large star*).

5. An amateurish performance might be done by someone who is a (*comedian, expert, novice*).

6. Someone who is <u>prudish</u> is (*reserved, flamboyant, easily embarrassed*).

7. A <u>brutish</u> comment might be made by someone who is (*humane, cautious, insensitive*).

8. If you find something <u>loathsome</u>, you find it (*obnoxious, engaging, pointless*).

9. If someone is <u>winsome</u>, they are not (*delightful, appealing, repulsive*).

10. You would (*read, reckon, refrigerate*) *a* <u>tabloid</u>.

For each boldface word, choose one synonym and one antonym. Put a circle around the synonym and underline the antonym.

11. **winsome**	a. appealing	b. conquering	c. unpleasant	d. breezy
12. **loathsome**	a. long-lasting	b. repugnant	c. attractive	d. lazy
13. **brutish**	a. cumbersome	b. mournful	c. sensitive	d. barbaric
14. **saintly**	a. wicked	b. healthy	c. pompous	d. virtuous
15. **amateurish**	a. envious	b. imperfect	c. polished	d. surprising

Conditional Words

Suffixes	Meanings	Words You Already Know
acy	*condition*	democr**acy**
tude	*condition*	atti**tude**
ure	*condition*	capt**ure**

New Words

Definitions	Sentences

accuracy (n) - state of being exactly truthful and free of errors; precision

Being an accountant requires <u>accuracy</u>.

aptitude (n) - a capacity or ability for anything; ability, readiness to learn

He showed an <u>aptitude</u> for playing the violin at a young age.

censure (n) - strong expression of disapproval; criticism

The punishment was meant to <u>censure</u> the peasants' actions.

forfeiture (n) - the state of losing some right, property, honor, or privilege as a penalty

His poor management of the business caused the <u>forfeiture</u> of the building and all the merchandise to his creditors.

immature (adj) - not mature; unripe or underdeveloped

Throwing a temper tantrum is <u>immature</u> behavior. You should be able to express your feelings without acting like a child.

lassitude (n) - lack of energy; exhaustion; weariness

Hot summer days bring on feelings of <u>lassitude</u>, and all I want to do is lay around and do nothing.

literacy (n) - the ability to read and write

<u>Literacy</u> is essential if you are going to get a good, well-paying job

lunacy (n) - insanity, craziness; frenzy; mental unsoundness

My brother's decision to quit his job is pure <u>lunacy</u>.

rapture (n) - state of being carried away with extreme joy; ecstasy; bliss

When I fell in love I was in a state of complete, unrestrained <u>rapture</u>.

solitude (n) - state of being alone; seclusion

Sometimes when I am really tired, I like to have complete <u>solitude</u> so I can rest and relax.

Conditional Words

Match each word on the left with the condition that it is associated with on the right.

1. ____ accuracy   a. youthful or undeveloped

2. ____ aptitude   b. disapproval or condemnation

3. ____ censure   c. fatigue or weariness

4. ____ forfeiture   d. elation and excitement

5. ____ immature   e. insanity or craziness

6. ____ lassitude   f. free from error

7. ____ literacy   g. isolation and privacy

8. ____ lunacy   h. learning and enlightenment

9. ____ rapture   i. ability or intelligence

10. ____ solitude   j. loss or penalty

Answer the following questions. Use the back of this piece of paper.

11. Name one task in which <u>accuracy</u> is important.

12. What is one thing for which you have an <u>aptitude</u>?

13. What are two things you would like to <u>censure</u>?

14. Give three reasons why <u>literacy</u> is important.

15. Describe what you like to do when you have total <u>solitude</u>.

States of Being

Suffixes	Meaning	Words You Already Know
ment	quality of, state of	content**ment**
ness	state of	loneli**ness**
tion, sion	state of, act of	celebra**tion**

New Words

Definitions	Sentences
amendment (n) - a change for the better; a correction; an improvement	The <u>amendment</u> to the constitution corrected problems with the original document.
bereavement (n) - the state of losing a friend or relative by death; deprivation; loss	Her <u>bereavement</u> after her husband's death left her depressed.
indictment (n) - the act of accusing of wrongdoing; to charge with a crime	The <u>indictment</u> came just three days after his arrest but months before the trial.
mustiness (n) - the odor or flavor of mold; stale moldy smell or taste	When we opened the door to the basement we were overcome with a foul <u>mustiness.</u>
preparedness (n) - the state of being prepared or ready, especially for war	The country's <u>preparedness</u> for war was not satisfactory, so it did not aggravate its enemies.
purification (n) - the act of removing pollution, impurities, contamination or guilt	In processing food, <u>purification</u> is one of the most important steps.
resentment (n) - strong feelings of anger because of insult or wrong; bitterness	Her feelings of <u>resentment</u> toward her sister prevented a close relationship.
seemliness (n) - the state of being fit or appropriate	The <u>seemliness</u> of the committee's actions were questioned by the citizens.
suspension (n) - the state of hanging; state of discontinuing something	The class's bad behavior resulted in the <u>suspension</u> of its gym privileges.
verification (n) - the act of checking the truth or correctness of something	Before signing a document, get <u>verification</u> that all the facts are correct.

I certify that all of ...
information is correct.

Signature Required

States of Being

Tell whether each statement is true or false.

1. **T F** If you feel resentful, you are quick to forgive and forget.

2. **T F** Purification involves a cleansing.

3. **T F** If you are experiencing bereavement, you will probably be feeling sorrowful.

4. **T F** Mustiness is a foul, unpleasant smell.

5. **T F** An amendment allows things to remain unaltered.

6. **T F** If you get verification, you get confirmation.

7. **T F** The seemliness of something depends on how it is sewn.

8. **T F** If you are in a state of preparedness, you are fit and ready.

9. **T F** An indictment is the same as an accusation.

10. **T F** A suspension of services means that it's business as usual.

Complete these analogies.

11. _____ : loss :: misfortune : hardship

12. resumption : _____ :: acquire : forfeit

13. forgiveness : mercifulness :: _____ : vengefulness

14. acquittal : _____ :: belief : suspicion

15. change : _____ :: status quo : sameness

More States of Being

Lesson 51

Suffixes	Meanings	Words You Already Know
ance, ancy	*state of*	hesit**ancy**, brilli**ance**
ence, ency	*state of*	resid**ence**
ity	*state of*	abil**ity**
ship	*state of*	hard**ship**

New Words

Definitions	Sentences
absurdity (n) - the state of being ridiculously unreasonable or nonsensical	*We all laughed at the <u>absurdity</u> of seeing the principal kiss a pig.*
acuity (n) - sharpness, especially referring to vision	*Few birds have the <u>acuity</u> of a hawk.*
competence (n) - the state of being capable or fit	*Her <u>competence</u> in her field was the reason she was promoted.*
complacency (n) - the state of being pleased or content with oneself; smugness	*Her <u>complacency</u> irked her mother, who wanted her daughter to always strive to do better.*
fatality (n) - a fixed, unalterable course of events; an event resulting in death	*The traffic <u>fatality</u> was the result of an intoxicated driver losing control of his car.*
fellowship (n) - an association with friends or other people with common interests	*Darcy enjoyed the <u>fellowship</u> of the other horseback riders.*
relevancy (n) - the state of being suitable or relating to the case at hand	*I don't see the <u>relevancy</u> of your argument. It doesn't relate to what we are discussing.*
reluctance (n) - unwillingness; not wanting to do something or agree with something	*James expressed <u>reluctance</u> to try out for the class play.*
sanctity (n) - the state of being sacred; holiness	*Speak quietly when you enter the church so you don't disturb the <u>sanctity</u> of the building.*
scholarship (n) - the quality of work done by a student; academic achievement	*Peter's <u>scholarship</u> was recognized with a medal and a certificate at the awards assembly.*

More States of Being

Match each word on the left with the word or phase on the right.

1. ____ absurdity   a. self-satisfaction or contentment

2. ____ acuity   b. sharpness or severity

3. ____ competence   c. camaraderie

4. ____ complacency   d. unwillingness or aversion

5. ____ fatality   e. sacredness

6. ____ fellowship   f. nonsense or unreasonableness

7. ____ relevancy   g. learning and wisdom

8. ____ reluctance   h. appropriateness

9. ____ sanctity   i. capability or fitness

10. ____ scholarship   j. terrible accident, death, or destiny

Use vocabulary words to complete these sentences.

11. The guests at the marriage ceremony were asked to respect the _____ of the ceremony by not taking flash pictures.

12. Do I sense a _____ on your part to volunteer to be president?

13. Years after John left college and his fraternity brothers he had fond memories of the _____ they shared.

14. While grandfather is 80 years old, his mental _____ would rival someone much younger.

15. Sometimes my father's discussions have no _____ to what I have requested. He talks about everything except the issue at hand.

People

Suffixes	Meaning	Words You Already Know
ar, er, or	*one who*	baker, actor, liar
ist	*one who*	artist, dentist

New Words

Definitions	Sentences
ancestor (n) - a person from whom one has descended	*She was proud that Winston Churchill was one of her ancestors.*
astronomer (n) - one who is trained in the science dealing with stars and planets	*The astronomer did most of her work at night when she could easily view the stars.*
chauvinist (n) - one who has a blind devotion to a certain cause	*He was such a chauvinist! He wouldn't even listen to another point of view.*
chronicler (n) - someone who records events and when they happened	*It was the job of the chronicler to record all the important events of the organization.*
conqueror (n) - one who gains control by force	*Alexander the Great was the conqueror of the Persian Empire.*
conspirator (n) - one who secretly plans with other people to perform an unlawful act	*While he was thought to be one of the conspirators, there was no evidence that he was a part of the terrorist group.*
linguist (n) - a person who is skilled in the study of language	*If you gave the linguist any word, she was able to tell you the word's complete history.*
narcissist (n) - one who exhibits abnormal interest in his or her own appearance and importance	*She got the reputation of being a narcissist because she was always looking at herself admiringly in the mirror.*
pessimist (n) - one who believes the world is bad or who looks on the dark side of life	*While Charlie is a pessimist, his wife is just the opposite. She looks on the bright side of things.*
proprietor (n) - someone who owns a business or property	*The proprietor of the business is the best person to talk to about getting a job.*

People

Choose the word or phrase that best describes or defines the first word.

1. **ancestor**
   descendant
   forefather
   procrastinator

2. **narcissist**
   self-centered
   fragrant
   humble

3. **conspirator**
   conspicuous
   submissive
   subversive

4. **conqueror**
   victor
   combat
   loser

5. **proprietor**
   manager
   owner
   tenant

6. **pessimist**
   Gloomy Gus
   Daddy Warbucks
   Mary Sunshine

7. **linguist**
   popular lecturer
   medical specialist
   language expert

8. **chauvinist**
   blind devotion
   level headed
   severe criticism

9. **astronomer**
   artifact digger
   star gazer
   record keeper

Use vocabulary words to complete these sentences.

10. From which _____ did you inherit your musical talent?

11. She was the city's official _____ and kept a record of all important events.

12. I don't like her because she is such a conceited _____ .

13. The _____ accepted the surrender of the leader of the defeated army.

14. He is a _____ when it comes to politics. He won't even listen to anyone else's
    ideas on the subject.

15. I don't know if she is always a _____ or if she is just feeling negative lately.

In the Making

Suffixes	Meanings	Words You Already Know
ate	to make	separ**ate**
en	to make	weak**en**
fy, ify	to make	terr**ify**
ize	to make	real**ize**

New Words

Definitions	Sentences
actualize (v) - to make real; to make happen	*You can <u>actualize</u> your dreams by working hard to make them real.*
diversify (v) - to make varied; to add variety	*I need to <u>diversify</u> the kinds of flowers in my yard so I don't have all yellow flowers.*
fabricate (v) - to build, manufacture or invent; to devise or create	*She was a master at <u>fabricating</u> mystery stories that no one could figure out until the very end.*
facilitate (v) - to make less difficult; to assist the progress of	*If you take my advice, it will <u>facilitate</u> your efforts to get a job.*
heighten (v) - to make higher or more intense; to increase or amplify	*The pep rally <u>heightened</u> the team's determination to win the homecoming game.*
mesmerize (v) - to charm or hypnotize; to enthrall; to overpower	*I was <u>mesmerized</u> by the beauty and grandeur of the palace ballroom.*
mitigate (v) - to reduce the force, intensity or painfulness; to calm	*Putting aloe salve on the burn will <u>mitigate</u> the pain.*
patronize (v) - to support or promote; to do business with	*I always try to <u>patronize</u> local stores instead of shopping in other towns.*
ventilate (v) - to bring in and circulate fresh air; to make widely known	*It's so stuffy in here. Could you open the door and <u>ventilate</u> this room?*
vilify (v) - to slander or defame; to speak ill of; to put down	*In the story, the villain's attempt to <u>vilify</u> the hero backfired on him.*

In the Making

Name

Choose the word in each line that means the same or nearly the same as the first word.

1. **actualize**   sharp   realize   fictitious
2. **diversify**   interrupt   sidetrack   vary
3. **fabricate**   destroy   construct   materialize
4. **facilitate**   assist   copy   hinder
5. **heighten**   elevate   degrade   measure
6. **mesmerize**   disenchant   merge   captivate
7. **mitigate**   increase   lessen   migrate
8. **patronize**   oppose   support   monitor
9. **ventilate**   close   modify   aerate
10. **vilify**   disgrace   villain   honor

Answer each of the following questions. Use the back of this paper.

11. Name two causes or organizations you <u>patronize</u>.

12. What would you like to <u>fabricate</u>?

13. Name a world-wide problem that you would like to <u>mitigate</u> and one thing you could do to help with this problem.

14. If you could <u>diversity</u> something, what would it be?

15. What do you wish someone would <u>facilitate</u> for you?

Related To

Suffixes	Meanings	Words You Already Know
ary	*related to, quality*	burgl**ary**
ery	*related to, quality*	brav**ery**
ory	*related to, quality*	mem**ory**

New Words

Definitions	Sentences
arbitrary (adj) - depending on someone's preference or whim; unreasonable	*I made an <u>arbitrary</u> decision that we would go to the park for the birthday party.*
bribery (n) - giving or taking rewards for acting or deciding in a certain way	*The official was accused of <u>bribery</u>, but there was no evidence that he was paid for his decision.*
cautionary (adj) - urging caution or care; related to a warning	*The train sounded a <u>cautionary</u> whistle before it approached the intersection.*
conciliatory (adj) - tending to make peace between people or gain good will	*The meeting opened with a <u>conciliatory</u> speech by the mediator.*
culinary (adj) - related to cooking or the kitchen	*My <u>culinary</u> skills are not very good, but I'm very skilled at gardening.*
drudgery (n) - hard, menial, unpleasant and boring work	*I deal with the <u>drudgery</u> of the task by taking little breaks from working.*
hereditary (adj) - passed down from an ancestor; transmitted from parent to child	*Some diseases are <u>hereditary</u>, so the tendency to have the disease can be passed to your children.*
laudatory (adj) - expressing praise	*The principal's <u>laudatory</u> letter congratulated the teacher on her good work.*
migratory (adj) - related to moving from one location to another	*The <u>migratory</u> habits of the Canadian geese take them to warmer climates for the winter.*
promissory (adj) - related to a promise	*I signed the <u>promissory</u> note saying that I would pay back the money plus interest.*

Related To

Choose the word or phrase that completes each sentence.

1. If you have <u>culinary</u> skills, you are good (*on the tennis court,   in the kitchen,   at school*).

2. A <u>cautionary</u> statement would give you (*a warning,   advice,   a greeting*).

3. If someone has <u>migratory</u> tendencies, they like to (*win,   wander,   whine*).

4. Your <u>hereditary</u> traits are things that are (*in your genes,   carried by germs,   a product of gluttony*).

5. You would really (*look forward to,   write about,   dread*) doing something you think is <u>drudgery</u>.

6. A <u>laudatory</u> statement expresses (*praise,   criticism,   jealousy*).

7. A <u>conciliatory</u> offer is one that attempts to (*pamper,   pacify,   perplex*).

8. <u>Bribery</u> usually involves (*an illegal gift,   a solemn ceremony,   a legal contract*).

9. A <u>promissory</u> speech would give people something to (*think about,   hope for,   gossip about*).

10. An <u>arbitrary</u> choice usually takes into consideration the opinions of (*everyone involved,   your closest advisors,   no one else*).

Tell whether the two words in each pair have the same or different meanings.

11. **laudatory — complimentary**   same   different

12. **hereditary — earned**   same   different

13. **arbitrary — subjective**   same   different

14. **conciliatory — antagonistic**   same   different

15. **migratory — nomadic**   same   different

Listing of Suffixes

Suffixes	Meaning	Sample Words
able, ible	*able, can do*	See Lesson 44
ac	*like*	cardiac, maniac, insomniac, artistic
acy	*condition*	See Lesson 49
age	*state of*	storage, savage, bondage, courage, marriage, pillage, wastage
al	*like, pertaining to*	See Lesson 45
an	*related to*	American, sylvan, urban, agrarian
ance, ancy	*state of*	See Lesson 51
ant	*one who*	servant, assistant, defendant, supplicant, participant
ar	*one who*	See Lesson 52
archy	*government*	anarchy, oligarchy
ary	*one who*	reactionary, revolutionary, dignitary, visionary, actuary, adversary, missionary, emissary, mercenary, secretary, beneficiary
ary	*related to, quality*	See Lesson 54
ary	*place where*	library, sanctuary, apothecary, estuary, dictionary, mortuary, sanctuary, seminary
ate	*to make*	See Lesson 53
cracy	*government*	democracy, theocracy
cule	*very small*	articulate, minuscule, ridicule, molecule, meticulous
en	*quality of*	golden, ashen
en	*to make*	See Lesson 53
ence, ency	*state of*	See Lesson 51
ent	*one who*	president, student, regent, resident
er	*one who*	See Lesson 52
ery	*place where*	bakery, bindery, cemetery, monastery, tannery, grocery, fishery, nunnery
ery	*practice, occupation*	surgery, robbery, archery, trickery, witchery
ery	*related to, quality*	See Lesson 54
fic	*causing*	beneficiary, horrific, pacific, personification, prolific, terrific, specific

Suffixes	Meaning	Sample Words
ful	*full of*	See Lesson 47
fy, ify	*to make*	See Lesson 53
hood	*state of*	nationhood, brotherhood, neighborhood, manhood
ia	*condition*	hysteria, hypothermia, anemia, pneumonia, mania
ible	*able, can do*	See Lesson 44
ic	*like, pertaining to*	See Lesson 46
ical	*like, pertaining to*	See Lesson 46
il, ile	*capable of being, like*	See Lesson 44
ine	*like, pertaining to*	See Lesson 45
ish	*like, resembling*	See Lesson 48
ism	*act of*	heroism, barbarism, despotism, plagiarism realism, romanticism, materialism
ist	*one who*	See Lesson 52
ity	*state of*	See Lesson 51
ive	*like, pertaining to*	See lesson 46
ize	*to make*	See Lesson 53
less	*without*	See Lesson 47
like	*like*	childlike, ladylike, lifelike, warlike
ling	*small*	darling, duckling, fledgling, hireling, inkling nestling, sapling, underling
ly	*like, resembling*	See Lesson 48
ment	*quality of, state of*	See Lesson 50
ness	*state of*	See Lesson 50
oid	*like, resembling*	See Lesson 48
ology	*study of*	etymology, ethnology, biology, anthropology, geology, theology, criminology, psychology, philosophy
or	*one who*	See Lesson 52
ory	*place where*	dormitory, reformatory, preparatory, depository, factory, territory, conservatory, observatory, laboratory, promontory
ory	*related to, quality*	See Lesson 54

Suffixes	Meaning	Sample Words
ose, ous	*full of, excessive*	See Lesson 47
ous	*like pertaining to*	See Lesson 45
ry	act of, state of	bigotry, revelry, perjury, rivalry, symmetry, citizenry, usury
ship	*state of*	See Lesson 51
sion	*act of, state of*	See Lesson 50
sis	*result of*	analysis, synthesis, conversion, suspension
some	*like, resembling*	See Lesson 48
tion	*act of, state of*	See Lesson 50
tude	*condition*	See Lesson 49
ure	*condition*	See Lesson 49
y	*inclined to*	arty, cheery, crafty, furry, dirty, dreary, foxy, icy, misty, rosy, savory, sleepy, slippery, sleepy, smelly, sunny, wealthy

Answers

Lesson 1 - Over and Under
1. translucent
2. transcribed
3. subdue
4. transplant
5. transfer
6. subsidize
7. subterranean
8. subconscious
9. subjugate
10. transformed
11. substitute - e
12. translate - d
13. subversive - a
14. transaction - b
15. subsequent - c

Lesson 2 - More, More, More
1. abundance
2. direct
3. ultimate
4. overstatement
5. fault-finding
6. tariff
7. c
8. d
9. b
10. a
11. hyperthermia
12. superimpose
13. surcharge
14. superlative
15. supervise

Lesson 3 - Before and After
1. precaution
2. preamble
3. forewarned
4. forethought
5. premature
6. posterior
7. premier
8. posthumous - e
9. forecast - c
10. postpone - i
11. premier - g
12. prejudice - d
13. forewarn - h
14. prevent - a
15. postdate - b
16. forerunner - f

Lesson 4 - Backward and Forward
1. delay
2. foreword
3. valley
4. past
5. backward
6. talent
7. past
8. declare publicly
9. launch
10. review
11. pro, profess
12. spect, retrospect
13. prologue, a book's introduction
14. retro, active, affecting the past
15. pensity, natural inclination

Lesson 5 - Around and Around
1. c
2. g
3. f
4. a
5. d
6. b
7. e
8. periscope
9. closest
10. circulatory
11. periodic
12. circumnavigate
13. periscope
14. periphery
15. circulatory
16. perigee

Lesson 6 - Ways to Move
1. abstract
2. detach
3. unique
4. whisper
5. induct
6. include
7. integrate
8. join in
9. borrow
10. diagonally
11. recurrent
12. secession
13. adjacent
14. adapt
15. seclude
16. reiterated

Lesson 7 - Coming Through
1. i
2. c
3. e
4. g
5. h
6. a
7. j
8. d
9. b
10. f
11. diagram - an explanatory picture
12. diagnose - identification of a disease
13. diaphanous - transparent
14. persist - not giving up
15. diameter - the distance across the center of a circle
16. dialect - a speech pattern

Lesson 8 - Outside
1. extruded
2. ecstasy
3. exodus
4. eccentric
5. excerpt
6. effusive
7. eject
8. effervesced
9. expulsion
10. emitted
11. eccentric - odd, abnormal
12. eject - throw out   13. expulsion - exile, removal
14. extraordinary - unusual, remarkable, unique
15. extraterrestrial - beyond earth
16. extend - stretch out, lengthen

Lesson 9 - All Together
1. e
2. g
3. d
4. i
5. a
6. c
7. b
8. h
9. f
10. j
11. disjointed
12. separated
13. segregate
14. asymmetry
15. counteract
16. disagreement

Lesson 10 - Moving Away
1. F
2. T
3. T
4. F
5. F
6. T
7. T
8. F
9. T
10. F
11. abstain
12. abstract
13. aboriginals
14. abdicate, abandon
15. absolved

Lesson 11 - Against

1. counter - i
2. obstinate - f
3. antiseptic - g
4. oblique - c
5. antagonist - a
6. obnoxious - h
7. obscure - e
8. counterbalance - j
9. contradiction- b
10. antisocial - d
11. antisocial
12. counterproductive
13. obstinate
14. contradiction
15. antiseptic
16. oblique

Lesson 12 - Numbers 1 - 4

1. c
2. a
3. f
4. e
5. d
6. b
7. answers will vary
8. c
9. f
10. e
11. d
12. a
13. b
14. answers will vary
15. c
16. d
17. a
18. b
19. answers will vary
20. c
21. d
22. a
23. b
24. answers will vary

Lesson 13 - Numbers 5 - 10

1. quintuplets
2. pentagram
3. answers will vary
4. hexagon
5. sextant
6. answers will vary
7. septennial
8. answers will vary
9. octagon
10. octave
11. answers will vary
12. decade
13. decathlon
14. decimeter
15. answers will vary

Lesson 14 - Beside, Between, Among

1. curse
2. fingernail
3. prologue
4. interrupt
5. immediately
6. novel
7. exception
8. intersecting
9. locomotion
10. contradict
11. paraphrase
12. epidemic
13. paradigm
14. epilogue
15. parable
16. intercede

Lesson 15 - Down and Away

1. telepathy
2. default
3. catacomb
4. depose
5. degrade
6. telemarket
7. catastrophe
8. catalyst
9. debark
10. telephoto
11. cata - e
12. de - a
13. cata - f
14. tele - b
15. de - c
16. televise - d

Lesson 16 - In and Into

1. same
2. different
3. same
4. different
9. same
10. different
11. intrastate
12. influx

Lesson 16, continued

5. different
6. same
7. different
8. different
13. embellish
14. inducted
15. introspection

Lesson 17 - The Size of Things

1. T
2. F
3. T
4. T
5. F
6. T
7. F
8. T
9. F
10. T
11. megalopolis ·
12. megalith ·
13. multinational ·
14. polychromatic ·
15. multifaceted ·
16. polytheistic .

Lesson 18 - Just Not

1. unnamed
2. abnormal
3. uneducated
4. unreasonable
5. unlikely
6. lifeless
7. blustery
8. uncontrollable
9. nothing
10. ridiculous
11. living - inanimate ·
12. normal - atypical ·
13. named - anonymous ·
14. anyone - nonentity ·
15. nice - inclement ·
16. logical - illogical ·
17. likely - improbable .

Lesson 19 - Bringing and Building

1. same
2. same
3. different
4. different
5. different
6. same
7. different
8. different
9. someone who carries things
10. to construct or build again
11. underlying framework or principles of something
12. - 16. answers will vary

Lesson 20 - Ways of Writing

1. calligraphy
2. conscripted
3. monograph
4. prescription
5. autobiography
6. transcript
7. inscriptions
8. epigrams
9. graphic
10. geography
11. T
12. F
13. F
14. T
15. T

Lesson 21 - Reaching the End

1. expand
2. unreliable
3. hesitate
4. commencement
5. decisive
6. limited
7. quenchable
8. drain
9. begin
10. terminate
11. determine
12. confine
13. indeterminable
14. infinite
15. definitive

Lesson 22 - Father, Mother, Birth

1. genesis
2. matri, the female leader of a family
3. expatriate
4. paternal
5. gen, study of heredity
6. maternity
7. matri, dignified, like a married woman
8. patrician
9. matrimony
10. genealogy

11. T	14. F
12. F	15. F
13. T	16. F

Lesson 23 - All Things Big and Small

1. d	7. e
2. f	8. a
3. h	9. c
4. j	10. g
5. i	11 - 15. answers will vary
6. b	

Lesson 24 - All About Work

1. cooperate	8. technology, technician
2. dispense	9. operable, laborious
3. strenuous	10. cooperated (or collaborated)
4. functional	11. distribute
5. reparation	12. tribute
6. commendation	13. retribution
7. specialist	

Lesson 25 - Just Asking

1. inquisition	7. derogatory
2. arrogant	8. questionable
3. derogate	9. inquest
4. acquisition	10. prerogative
5. inquisitive	11 - 15. answers will vary
6. quest	

Lesson 26 - Life and Death

1. nation	9. healthy
2. guilt	10. embarrass
3. dull (or similar word)	11. international
4. sophisticated	12. vivacious
5. born	13. innate
6. lively	14. naive
7. born	15. remorse
8. life	

Lesson 27 - Earth and Sea

1. yes	6. no
2. no	7. yes
3. no	8. yes
4. no	9. no
5. yes	10. yes

Lesson 27, continued

Water or Sea - aquatic, maritime, dehydrate, hydraulic, marina, answers will vary for extra words

Land or Earth - geology, terrestrial, terrain, geothermal, subterranean, answers will vary for extra words

Lesson 28 - Some Body Words

1. bacteria, decompose	9. blood, cells
2. life, story	10. together, living
3. life-like, devices	11. corporation
4. atmosphere, life-giving	12. symbiosis
5. killing, mass	13. biodegradable
6. eat, meat	14. carnivorous
7. association, legal	15. bionic
8. overweight, stout	

Lesson 29 - Body Parts

1. manipulated	9. accord
2. maneuver	10. cardiac
3. capitulated	11. agreement, conflict
4. expedite	12. surrender, triumph
5. decapitate	13. friendly, disagreeable
6. pedestrian	14. speed up, hinder
7. cordial	15. obstruction, assistance
8. impediment	

Lesson 30 - Moving

1. f	9. e
2. j	10. g
3. a	11. concurrently
4. c	12. regressed
5. h	13. motivation
6. i	14. digress
7. d	15. cursory
8. b	

Lesson 31 - Look and See

1. hidden	9. spectrum
2. fictitious	10. envision
3. clear	11. kaleidoscope
4. exception	12. conspicuous
5. onlooker	13. perspective
6. eyesight	14. vista
7. inspection	15. speculating
8. imagine	

Lesson 32 - Speaking

1. verify	9. contestable
2. order	10. dictate
3. commandment	11. testimonial
4. articulate	12. T
5. tribute	13. F
6. talkative	14. F
7. commendation	15. T
8. indictment	

Lesson 33 - Sound Words

1. hearing
2. poem
3. harmony
4. loud enough
5. speech sounds
6. under water
7. playing records
8. try out
9. play instruments
10. rich and resonant
11. c. perceivable
12. d. agreement
13. e. tryout
14. b. concert
15. a. resounding

Lesson 34 - The Shape of Things

1. orb
2. hemisphere
3. atmosphere
4. spherical
5. rectitude
6. directive
7. cyclones
8. exorbitant
9. rectify
10. cyclical
11. correct
12. globular
13. dictum
14. excessive
15. good character
16. air

Lesson 35 - Strength and Power

1. fortify
2. potent
3. valid
4. dynamo
5. valorous
6. omnipotent
7. fortitude
8. dynamic
9. valor
10. dynasty
11. same
12. same
13. different
14. same
15. different
16. different

Lesson 36 - It's About Time

1. synchronize
2. diary
3. chronologically or chronological order
4. annual
5. chronic
6. extemporaneous
7. biennially
8. contemporary
9. journalism
10. annuity
11. physical exam
12. pain
13. historic events
14. currents news events
15. speaking

Lesson 37 - Twisting and Turning

1. e
2. i
3. a
4. j
5. b
6. d
7. h
8. g
9. c
10. f
11. conversant
12. adversary
13. aversion
14. versatile
15. torturous

Lesson 38 - Thinking and Remembering

1. memorialize
2. ancient
3. mental
4. analyze
5. understandable
6. souvenir
7. life story
8. feeling
9. practical
10. thin-skinned
11. memoir
12. sensation
13. intellectual
14. commemorate
15. sensible

Lesson 39 - Going, Going, Gone

1. proceed
2. precede
3. concede
4. access
5. procession
6. precedent
7. migratory
8. immigrants
9. secede
10. emigrant
11. immigrant
12. secede
13. procession
14. precede
15. concede

Lesson 40 - Take a Stand

1. stubborn
2. hinder
3. constant
4. shorter
5. fall
6. relentless
7. stop
8. staying the same
9. stands still
10. physical staying power
11. detour
12. flexible
13. weakness
14. dynamic
15. fickle

Lesson 41 - Touching and Holding

1. answers will vary
2. answers will vary
3. answers will vary
4. F
5. F
6. T
7. T
8. F
9. F
10. F
11. e. transmittable
12. a. tangent
13. d. keep up
14. b. persevering
15. c. diplomacy

Lesson 42 - Governmental Words

1. autocrat
2. dominion
3. fidelity
4. aristocracy
5. confidential
6. h
7. i
8. a
9. g
10. b
11. j
12. e
13. c
14. f
15. d

Lesson 43 - People

1. rock
2. temple
3. ruthless
4. merciless
5. solitary
6. wealth
7. peasants
8. fuse
9-12. answers will vary
13. F
14. T
15. F

Lesson 44 - Able and Capable

1. religious
2. sanitary
3. concrete
4. absorbent
5. irrational
6. peaceful
7. docile
8. edible
9. laughable
10. futile
11. e
12. d
13. b
14. c
15. a

Lesson 45 - It's Like

1. same
2. different
3. same
4. same
5. different
6. same
7. same
8. different
9. different
10. same
11. F
12. F
13. T
14. T
15. F

Lesson 46 - More Like Words

1. hysterical
2. affirmative
3. prolific
4. simplistic
5. barbaric
6. critical
7. objective
8. rustic
9. cohesive
10. evocative
11. answers will vary
12. answers will vary
13. answers will vary
14. answers will vary
15. answers will vary

Lesson 47 - With and Without

1. verbose
2. effortless
3. morose
4. pitiful
5. doubtful
6. merciful, vengeful
7. joyless
8. dutiful
9. bellicose
10. d
11. e
12. b
13. a
14. f
15. c

Lesson 48 - Resembling

1. pious
2. amiable
3. humans
4. small planet
5. novice
6. reserved
7. insensitive
8. obnoxious
9. repulsive
10. read
11. appealing, unpleasant
12. repugnant, attractive
13. barbaric, sensitive
14. virtuous, wicked
15. imperfect, polished

Lesson 49 - Conditional Words

1. f
2. i
3. b
4. j
5. a
6. c
7. h
8. e
9. d
10. g
11. answers will vary
12. answers will vary
13. answers will vary
14. answers will vary
15. answers will vary

Lesson 50 - States of Being

1. F
2. T
3. T
4. T
5. F
6. T
7. F
8. T
9. T
10. F
11. bereavement
12. suspension
13. resentment
14. indictment
15. amendment

Lesson 51 - More States of Being

1. f
2. b
3. i
4. a
5. j
6. c
7. h
8. d
9. e
10. g
11. sanctity
12. reluctance
13. fellowship
14. acuity
15. relevancy

Lesson 52 - People

1. forefather
2. self-centered
3. subversive
4. victor
5. owner
6. Gloomy Gus
7. language expert
8. blind devotion
9. star gazer
10. ancestor
11. chronicler
12. narcissist
13. conqueror
14. chauvinist
15. pessimist

Lesson 53 - In the Making

1. realize
2. vary
3. construct
4. assist
5. elevate
6. captivate
7. lessen
8. support
9. aerate
10. disgrace
11. answers will vary
12. answers will vary
13. answers will vary
14. answers will vary
15. answers will vary

Lesson 54 - Related To

1. in the kitchen
2. a warning
3. wander
4. in your genes
5. dread
6. praise
7. pacify
8. an illegal gift
9. hope for
10. no one else
11. same
12. different
13. same
14. different
15. same